Book and CD for B♭, E♭, C and Bass Clef Instruments

volume 84

Produced and Arranged by
Mark Taylor & Jim Roberts

10 LATIN FAVORITES

BOOK

CD

ISBN 978-1-4234-5296-6

7777 W. Bluemound Rd. P.O. Box 13819 Milwaukee, WI 53213

Visit Hal Leonard Online at
www.halleonard.com

BOSSA NOVA CLASSICS

Volume 84

Produced and Arranged by Mark Taylor & Jim Roberts

Featured Players:

Graham Breedlove-Trumpet
John Desalme-Saxophones
Tony Nalker-Piano
Jim Roberts-Bass
Dave McDonald-Drums

Recorded at Bias Studios, Springfield, Virginia
Bob Dawson, Engineer

HOW TO USE THE CD:

Each song has two tracks:

1) Split Track/Melody

Woodwind, Brass, Keyboard, and **Mallet Players** can use this track as a learning tool for melody style and inflection.

Bass Players can learn and perform with this track – remove the recorded bass track by turning down the volume on the LEFT channel.

Keyboard and **Guitar Players** can learn and perform with this track – remove the recorded piano part by turning down the volume on the RIGHT channel.

2) Full Stereo Track

Soloists or **Groups** can learn and perform with this accompaniment track with the RHYTHM SECTION only.

CD

C VERSION

BOSSA ANTIGUA

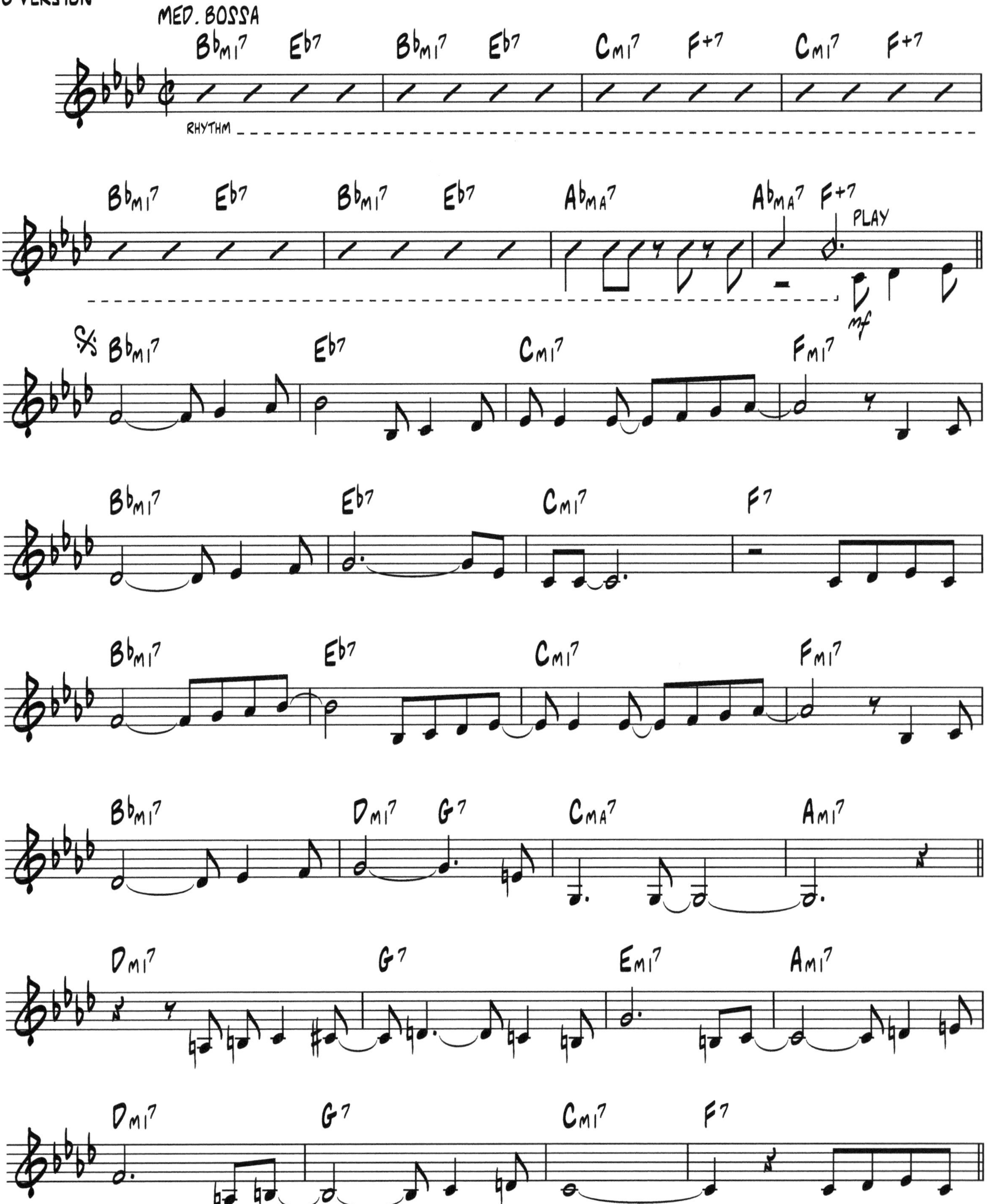

BY PAUL DESMOND

MED. BOSSA

RHYTHM

PLAY

B♭mi7 E♭7 Cmi7 Fmi7
B♭mi7 E♭7 A♭ma7 F+7
TO CODA
SOLO
B♭mi7 E♭7 Cmi7 Fmi7 B♭mi7
1.
E♭7
Cmi7 F7
2.
Dmi7 G7 Cma7 Ami7
Dmi7 G7 Emi7 Ami7 Dmi7 G7
Cmi7 F7 B♭mi7 E♭7 Cmi7 Fmi7
D.S. AL CODA
B♭mi7 E♭7 A♭ma7 B♭mi7 E♭7
CODA
B♭mi7 E♭7 B♭mi7 E♭7 Cmi7 F+7 Cmi7 F+7
B♭mi7 E♭7 B♭mi7 E♭7 A♭ma7

CD

ESTATE

MUSIC BY BRUNO MARTINO
LYRICS BY BRUNO BRIGHETTI

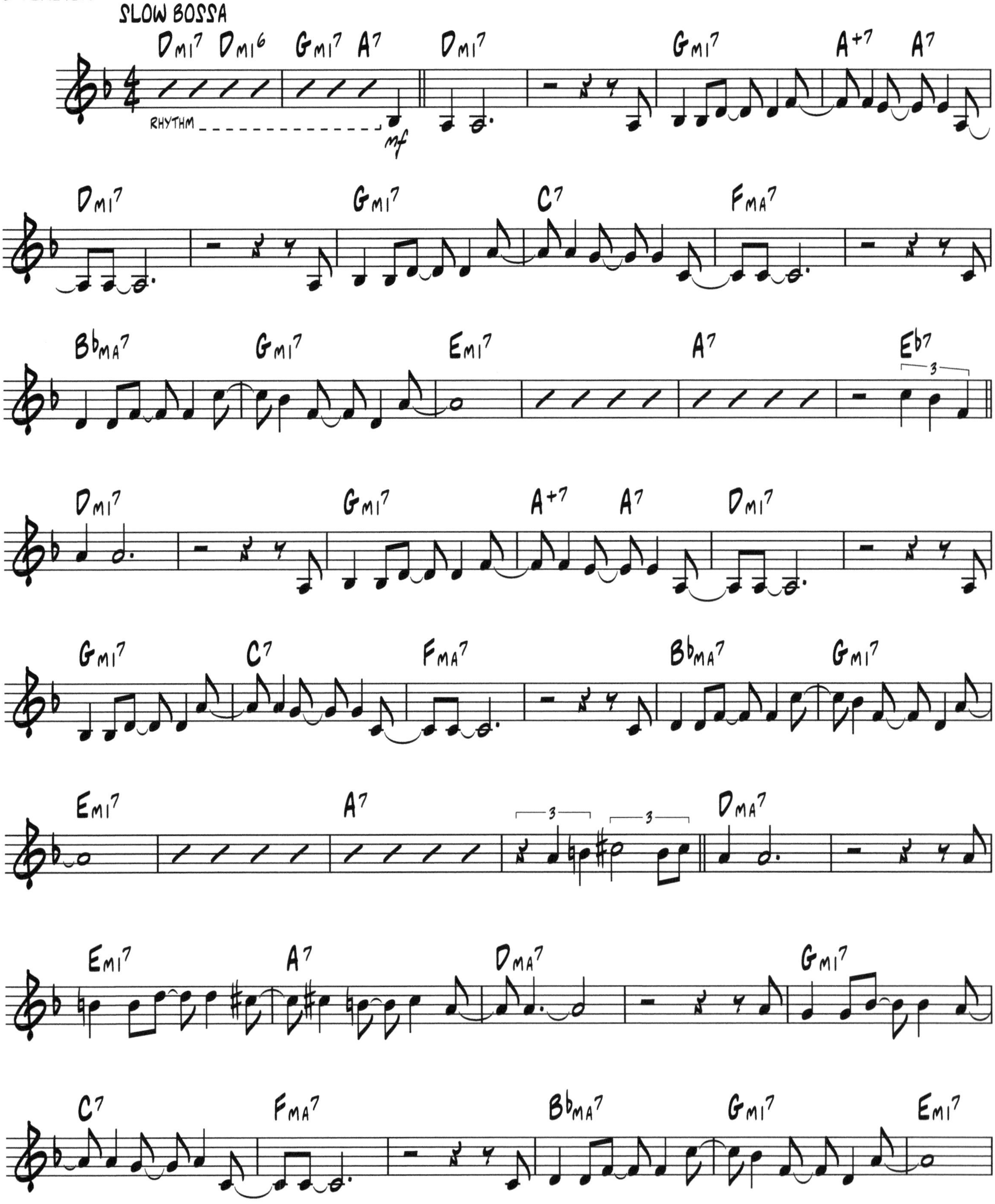

SLOW BOSSA

A7 Eb7 DMI7 GMI7
A+7 A7 DMI7 GMI7 C7
FMA7 BbMA7 GMI7 EMI7
A7 Eb7 DMI7 DMI6 GMI7 A7
DMI7 DMI6 BbMA7 GMI7 Eb7 SOLO DMA7 EMI7
A7 DMA7 GMI7 C7 FMA7 BbMA7
GMI7 EMI7 A7 Eb7 DMI7 GMI7
A+7 A7 DMI7 GMI7 C7 FMA7 BbMA7
GMI7 EMI7 A7 Eb7 DMI7 DMI6 GMI7
A7 DMI7 DMI6 GMI7 A7 DMI7

CD

7: SPLIT TRACK/MELODY

8: FULL STEREO TRACK

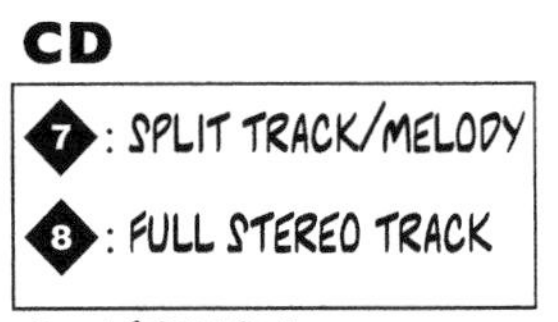

A FELICIDADE

WORDS AND MUSIC BY VINICIUS DE MORAES,
ANDRE SALVET AND ANTONIO CARLOS JOBIM

C VERSION

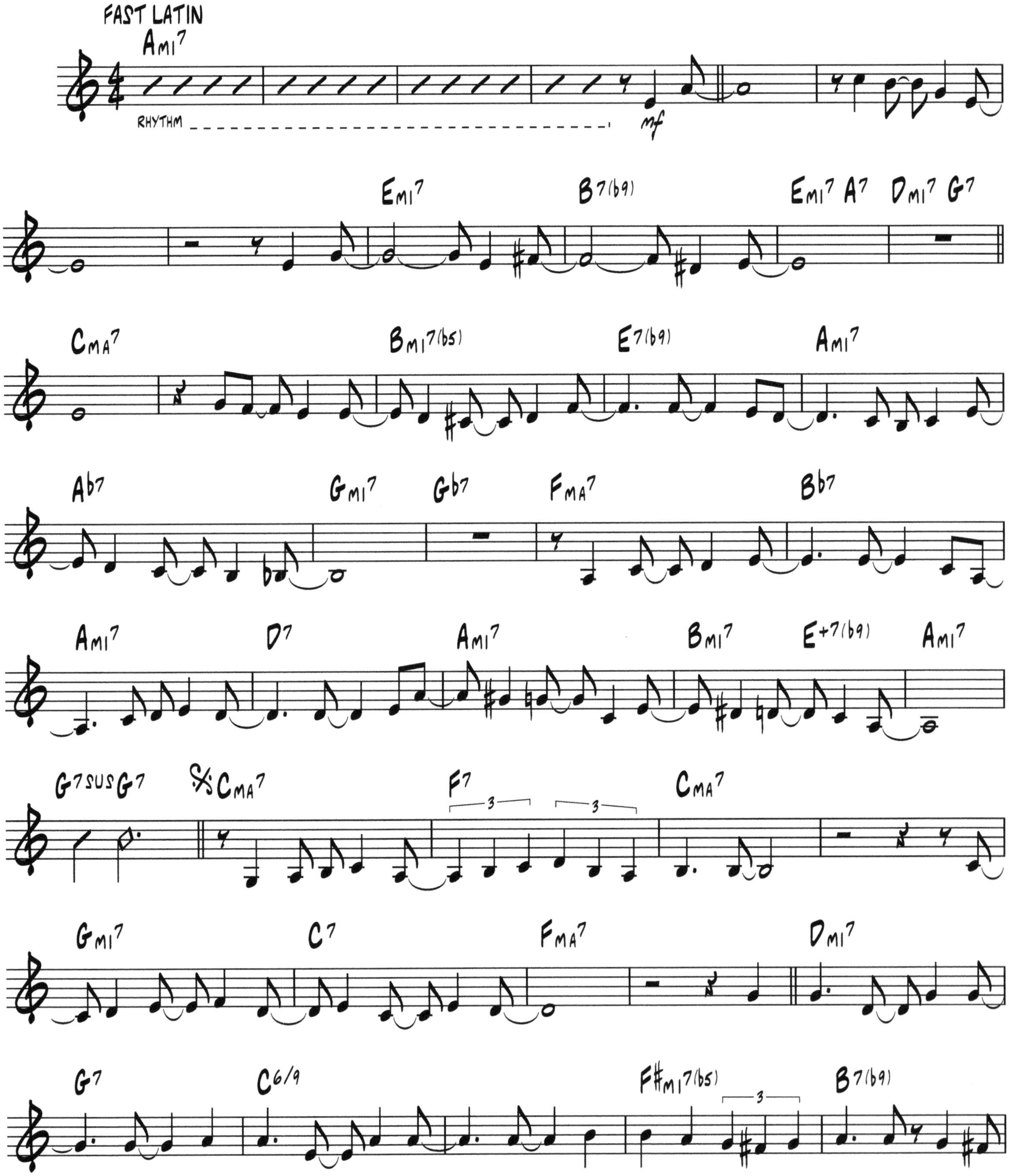

FAST LATIN
AMI7
RHYTHM
mf
EMI7
B7(b9)
EMI7 A7 DMI7 G7
CMA7
BMI7(b5)
E7(b9)
AMI7
Ab7
GMI7
Gb7
FMA7
Bb7
AMI7
D7
AMI7
BMI7
E+7(b9)
AMI7
G7SUS G7
CMA7
F7
3
3
CMA7
GMI7
C7
FMA7
DMI7
G7
C6/9
F#MI7(b5)
3
B7(b9)

EMI7 A7 DMI7 G7(b9) AMI7 AMI7/G D7/F#
TO CODA
DMI7/F AMI7 BMI7(b5) E+7(b9) AMI7
SOLO
EMI7 B7(b9) EMI7 A7 DMI7 G7
CMA7 BMI7(b5) E7(b9) AMI7 Ab7 GMI7 Gb7
FMA7 Bb7 AMI7 D7 AMI7 BMI7 E+7(b9) AMI7
G7SUS G7 CMA7 F7 CMA7 GMI7 C7
FMA7 DMI7 G7 C6/9 F#MI7(b5)
B7(b9) EMI7 A7 DMI7 G7(b9) AMI7 AMI7/G D7/F# DMI7/F
AMI7 BMI7(b5) E+7(b9) AMI7 G7SUS G7
D.S. AL CODA
CODA
PLAY 3X'S
AMI7
BMI7(b5) E+7(b9)
1., 2.
AMI7
3.
AMI7

CD

9: SPLIT TRACK/MELODY
10: FULL STEREO TRACK

FLAMINGO

C VERSION

LYRIC BY ED ANDERSON
MUSIC BY TED GROUYA

SOLO
CMA7 G7SUS G7(b9) CMA7 DMI7 G+7
CMI7 F7SUS F7 Ab7 G7SUS G7(b9)
1. CMA7 G7SUS G7(b9)
2. C6 GMI7 C+7
FMI7 Bb7 Eb6/9 E°7
FMI7 Bb7 /Ab G7SUS G7(b9) G+7(b9)
CMA7 DMI7 G+7 CMI7 Gb7 F7SUS F7
D.S. AL CODA
Ab7 G7SUS G7(b9) CMA7 GMI7 C+7
CODA
CMA7 Bb7 CMA7
Bb7 CMA7 Bb7 CMA7

CD
11: SPLIT TRACK/MELODY
12: FULL STEREO TRACK

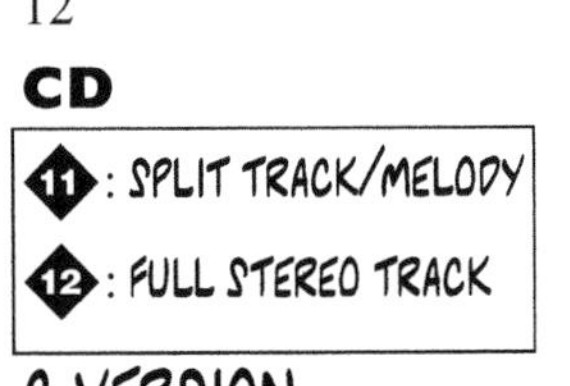

FRENESÍ

WORDS AND MUSIC BY
ALBERTO DOMINGUEZ

C VERSION

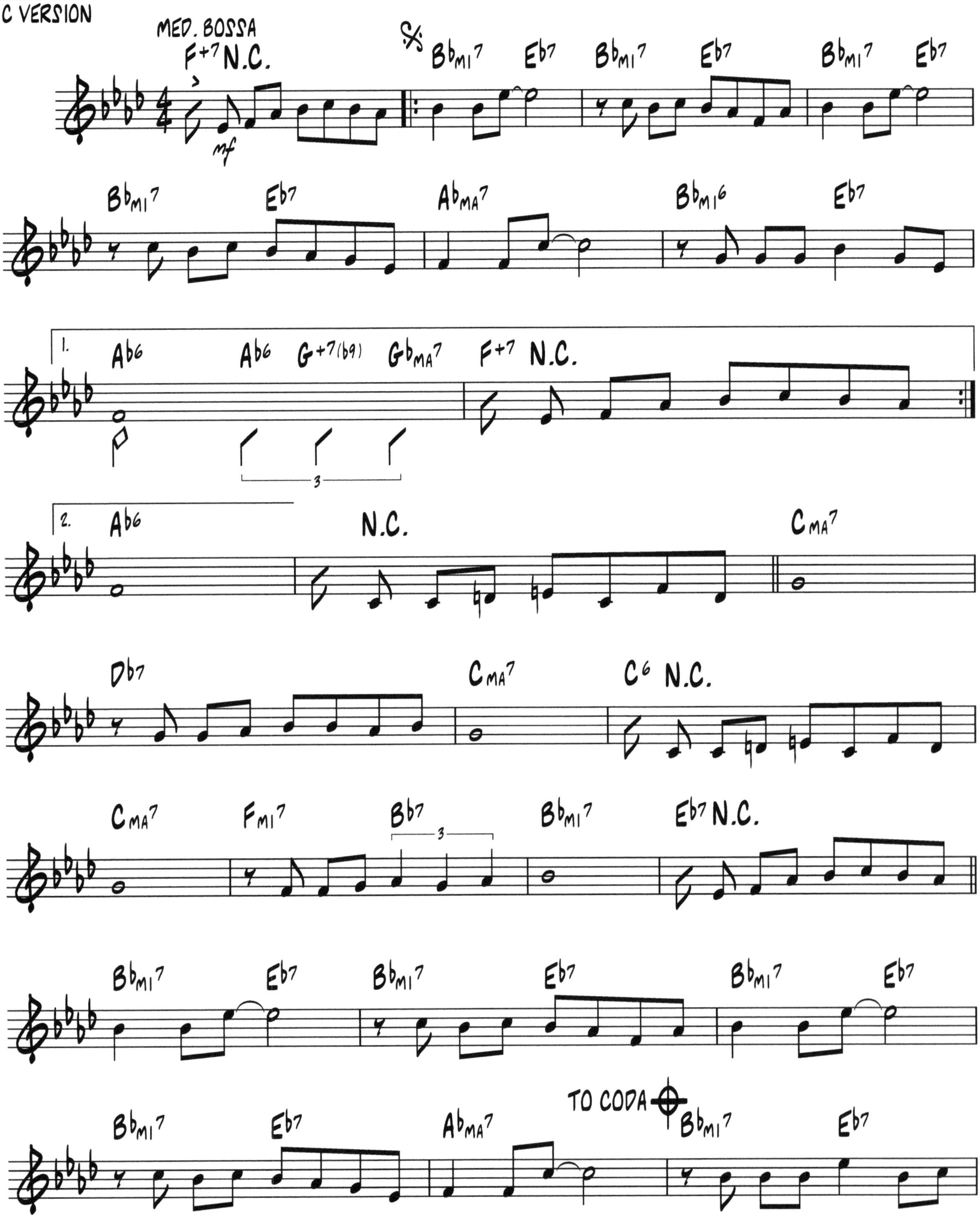

MED. BOSSA
F+7 N.C.
Bbmi7 Eb7 Bbmi7 Eb7 Bbmi7 Eb7
mf
Bbmi7 Eb7 Abma7 Bbmi6 Eb7
1. Ab6 Ab6 G+7(b9) Gbma7 F+7 N.C.
3
2. Ab6 N.C. Cma7
Db7 Cma7 C6 N.C.
Cma7 Fmi7 Bb7 Bbmi7 Eb7 N.C.
3
Bbmi7 Eb7 Bbmi7 Eb7 Bbmi7 Eb7
Bbmi7 Eb7 Abma7 TO CODA Bbmi7 Eb7

SOLO
Ab6 Ab6 G+7(b9) GbMA7 F+7 SOLO BREAK
Bbmi7 Eb7
Bbmi7 Eb7 Bbmi7 Eb7 Bbmi7 Eb7
AbMA7 Bbmi6 Eb7
1. Ab6 Ab6 G+7(b9) GbMA7
F+7
2. Ab6
CMA7 Db7 CMA7 C6
CMA7 Fmi7 Bb7 Bbmi7 Eb7
Bbmi7 Eb7 Bbmi7 Eb7 Bbmi7 Eb7 Bbmi7 Eb7 AbMA7
Bbmi7 Eb7 Ab6 Ab6 G+7(b9) GbMA7 F+7 N.C.
D.S. AL CODA
TAKE REPEAT
CODA
Bbmi7 A9(#11) AbMA7

CD

13: SPLIT TRACK/MELODY

14: FULL STEREO TRACK

HO-BA-LA-LA

WORDS AND MUSIC BY NORMAN GIMBEL
AND JOAO GILBERTO

C VERSION

TO CODA
AMI7
D7
G6
BMI7(b5) E+7(b9)
SOLO
AMI7
D7
D#o7
EMI7
Bb7
AMI7
D7
1.
BMI7(b5)
E+7(b9)
2.
G6
Db7
CMI7
F7
BbMA7
Bo7
CMI7
F7
AMI7
D7
BMI7(b5)
E+7(b9)
AMI7
D7
D#o7
EMI7
Bb7
AMI7
D7
G6
Bb7
D.S. AL CODA
CODA
CMA7
Bb7
CMA7
Bb7
CMA7
Bb7
CMA7
Bb7
GMA7
RIT.

MENINA FLOR

WORDS BY MARIA TOLEDO
MUSIC BY LUIZ BONFA

C VERSION

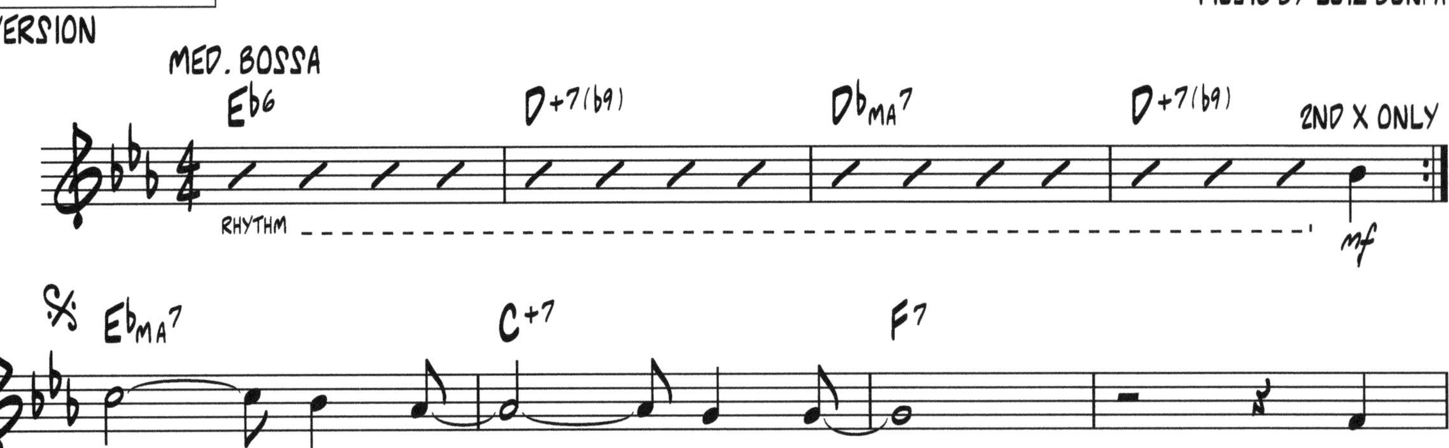

TO CODA
FMI7 Bb7SUS Bb7 Eb6 FMI7 Bb7
SOLOS (2 CHORUSES)
EbMA7 C+7 F7 FMI7 AbMI6
GMI7 C7 FMI7 Bb7 EbMA7 D7(b9) GMA7 G#o7
AMI7 D7 GMA7 FMI7 Bb7 EbMA7 C+7
F7 FMI7 AbMI6 GMI7 C7(b9)
FMI7 AbMI6 GMI7 CMI7
D.S. AL CODA
FMI7 Bb7SUS Bb7 Eb6 FMI7 Bb7
2ND X ONLY
CODA
Eb6 D+7(b9) DbMA7 D+7(b9)
Eb6 D+7(b9) DbMA7 D+7(b9) Eb6

CD

17 : SPLIT TRACK/MELODY

18 : FULL STEREO TRACK

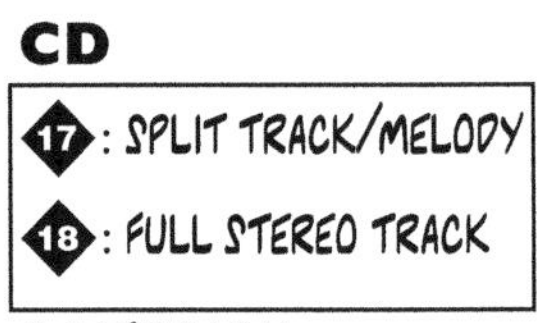

C VERSION

O PATO
(THE DUCK)

WORDS AND MUSIC BY JAYME SILVA AND NEUZA TEIXIERA
ENGLISH LYRIC BY JON HENDRICKS

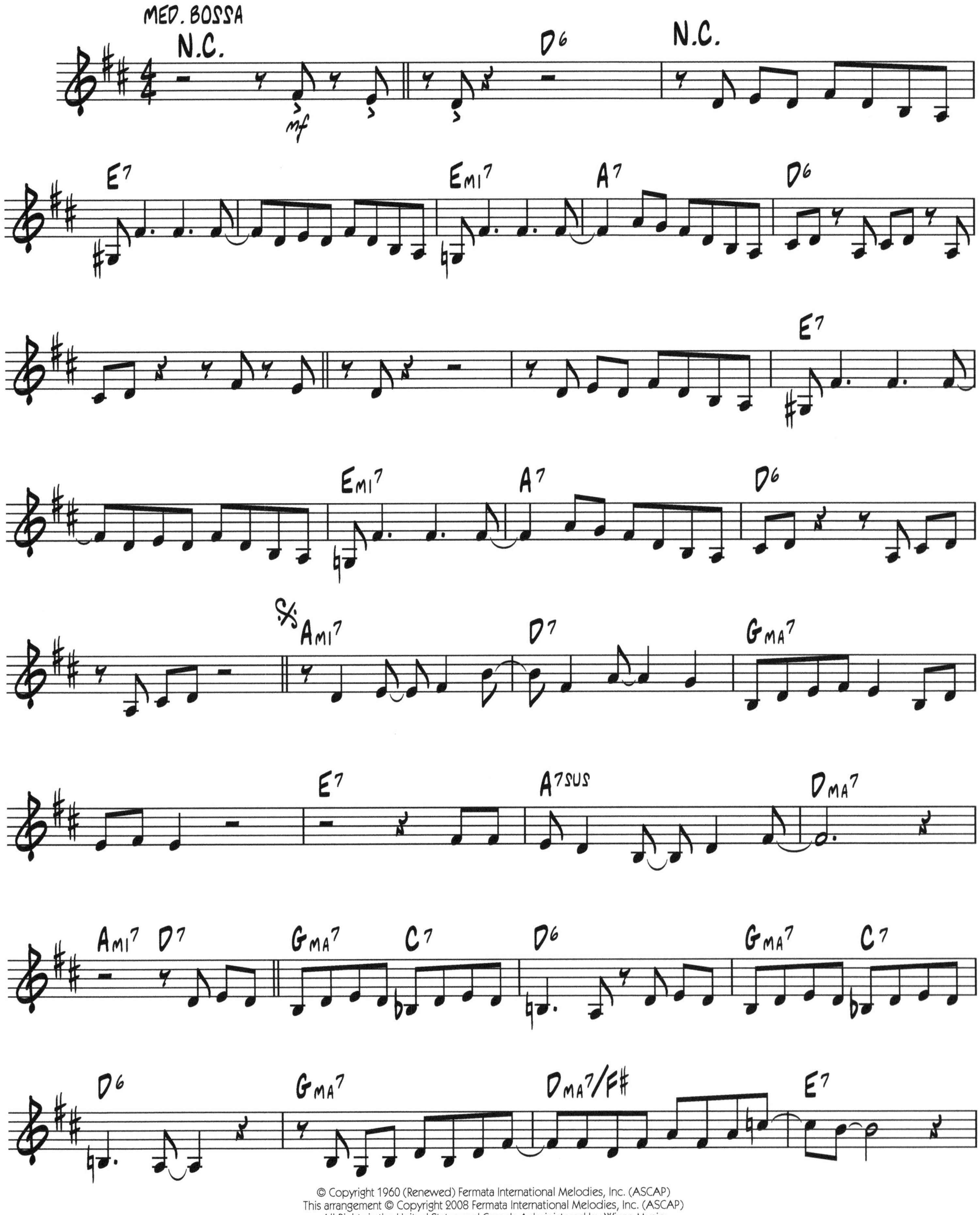

MED. BOSSA
N.C.
mf
D6
N.C.
E7
Emi7
A7
D6
E7
Emi7
A7
D6
Ami7
D7
Gma7
E7
A7sus
Dma7
Ami7
D7
Gma7
C7
D6
Gma7
C7
D6
Gma7
Dma7/F#
E7

A7
DMA7
E7
TO CODA
Eb7
D6 SOLO BREAK
SOLOS (2 FULL CHORUSES)
D6
E7
EMI7
A7
D6
AMI7
D7
GMA7
E7
A7SUS
DMA7
AMI7
D7
GMA7
C7
D6
GMA7
C7
D6
GMA7
DMA7/F#
E7
A7
DMA7
E7
Eb7(#9)
D6
D.S. AL CODA
CODA
Eb7
Bb+7
A7(b9)
D6

CD

19 : SPLIT TRACK/MELODY

20 : FULL STEREO TRACK

PETITE FLEUR
(LITTLE FLOWER)

BY SIDNEY BECHET

C VERSION

TO CODA
Ami7(b5)
Eb7
D7(b9)
Gmi7
D+7(b9)
SOLO
Ami7(b5)
D7(b9)
Gmi7
C7
Emi7(b5)
A7(b9)
Ami7(b5)
D+7(b9)
Ami7(b5)
D7(b9)
BbMA7
B°7
Cmi7
F7
BbMA7
Bb6
Ami7(b5)
D7(b9)
Gmi7
C7
Emi7(b5)
A7(b9)
Ami7(b5)
D+7(b9)
Ami7(b5)
D7(b9)
Gmi7
C7
Ami7(b5)
Eb7
D7(b9)
Gmi7
D+7(b9)
D.S. AL CODA
CODA
Gmi7
C7
FMA7
EbMA7
Ami7(b5)
Ami7(b5)/D
Gmi7

CD

1 : SPLIT TRACK/MELODY

2 : FULL STEREO TRACK

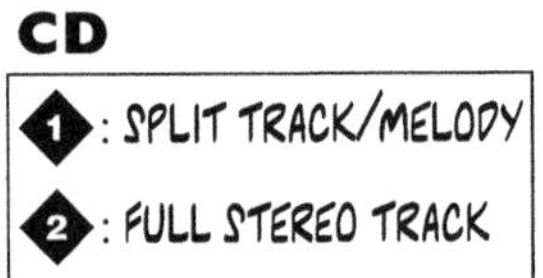

BIM-BOM

WORDS AND MUSIC BY
JOAO GILBERTO

C VERSION

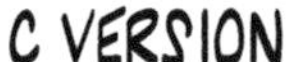

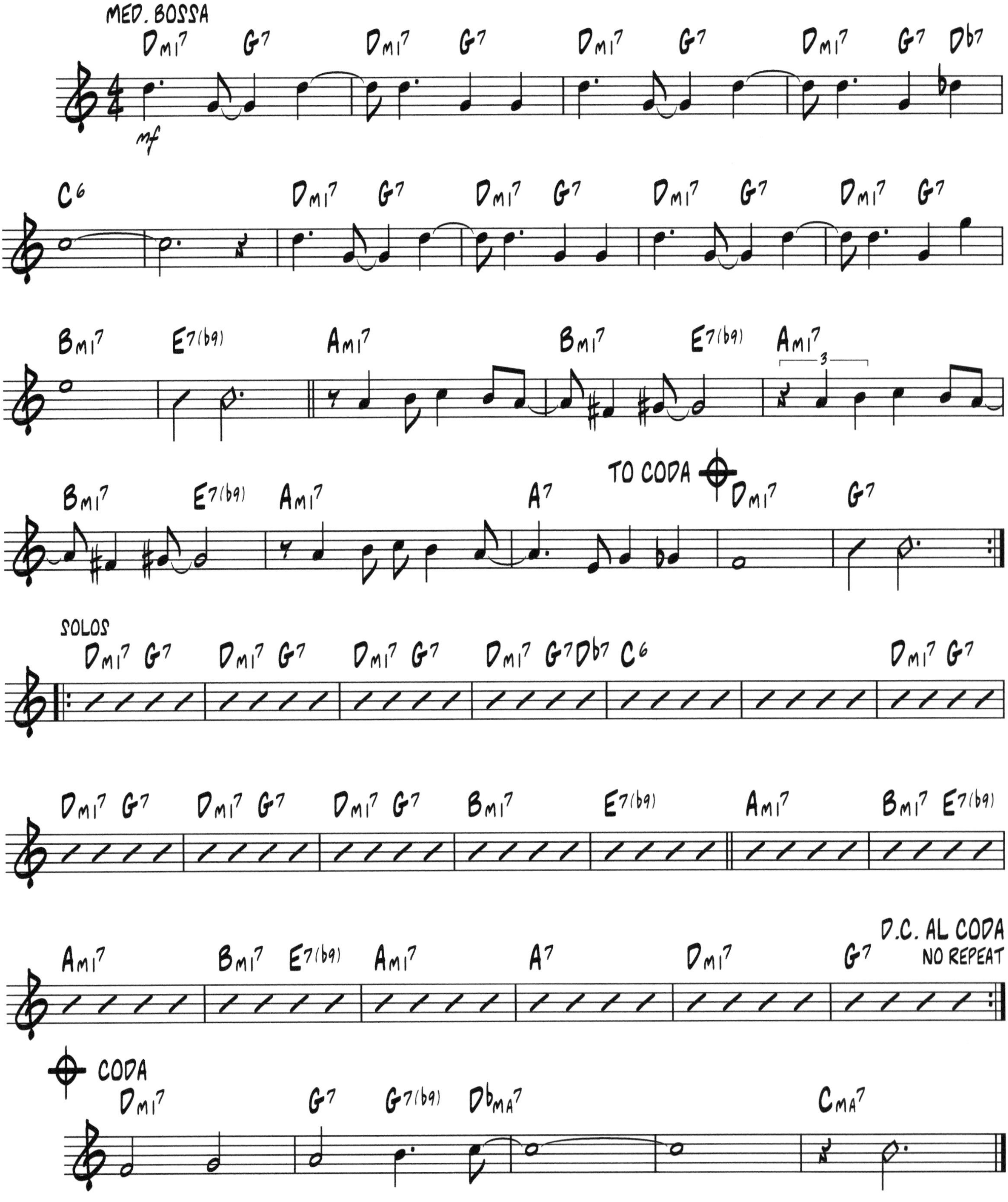

MED. BOSSA
Dmi7 G7 Dmi7 G7 Dmi7 G7 Dmi7 G7 Db7
mf
C6 Dmi7 G7 Dmi7 G7 Dmi7 G7 Dmi7 G7
Bmi7 E7(b9) Ami7 Bmi7 E7(b9) Ami7
3
Bmi7 E7(b9) Ami7 A7
TO CODA
Dmi7 G7
SOLOS
Dmi7 G7 Dmi7 G7 Dmi7 G7 Dmi7 G7 Db7 C6 Dmi7 G7
Dmi7 G7 Dmi7 G7 Dmi7 G7 Bmi7 E7(b9) Ami7 Bmi7 E7(b9)
D.C. AL CODA
NO REPEAT
Ami7 Bmi7 E7(b9) Ami7 A7 Dmi7 G7
CODA
Dmi7 G7 G7(b9) DbmA7 CmA7

BIM BOM

CD
1 : SPLIT TRACK/MELODY
2 : FULL STEREO TRACK
WORDS AND MUSIC BY
JOAO GILBERTO
Bb VERSION
MED. BOSSA
Emi7 A7 Emi7 A7 Emi7 A7 Emi7 A7 Eb7
mf
D6 Emi7 A7 Emi7 A7 Emi7 A7 Emi7 A7
C#mi7 F#7(b9) Bmi7 C#mi7 F#7(b9) Bmi7
3
C#mi7 F#7(b9) Bmi7 B7
TO CODA
Emi7 A7
SOLOS
Emi7 A7 Emi7 A7 Emi7 A7 Emi7 A7 Eb7 D6 Emi7 A7
Emi7 A7 Emi7 A7 Emi7 A7 C#mi7 F#7(b9) Bmi7 C#mi7 F#7(b9)
Bmi7 C#mi7 F#7(b9) Bmi7 B7 Emi7 A7
D.C. AL CODA
NO REPEAT
CODA
Emi7 A7 A7(b9) Ebma7 Dma7

CD

3: SPLIT TRACK/MELODY
4: FULL STEREO TRACK

BOSSA ANTIGUA

BY PAUL DESMOND

B♭ VERSION

CMI7 F7 DMI7 GMI7
CMI7 F7 B♭MA7 G+7
TO CODA
SOLO
CMI7 F7 DMI7 GMI7 CMI7
1.
F7
DMI7 G7
2.
EMI7 A7 DMA7 BMI7
EMI7 A7 F♯MI7 BMI7 EMI7 A7
DMI7 G7 CMI7 F7 DMI7 GMI7
D.S. AL CODA
CMI7 F7 B♭MA7 CMI7 F7
CODA
CMI7 F7 CMI7 F7 DMI7 G+7 DMI7 G+7
CMI7 F7 CMI7 F7 B♭MA7

CD
5: SPLIT TRACK/MELODY
6: FULL STEREO TRACK

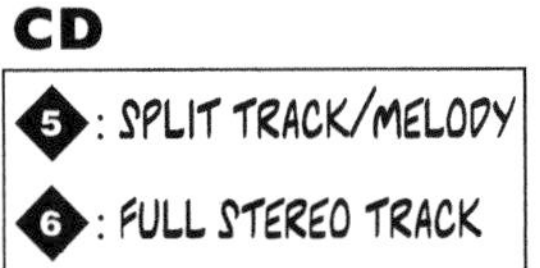

ESTATE

MUSIC BY BRUNO MARTINO
LYRICS BY BRUNO BRIGHETTI

Bb VERSION

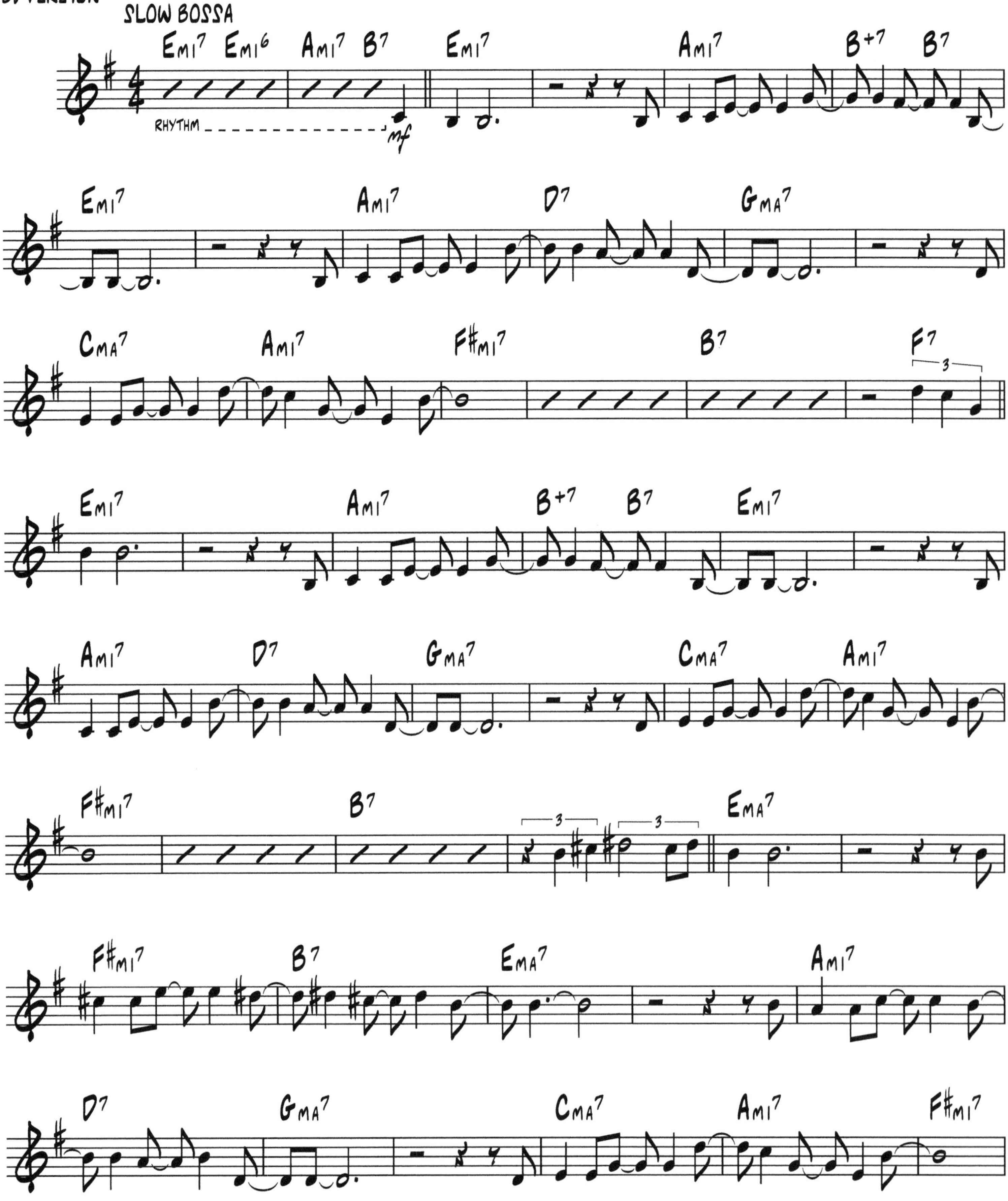

SLOW BOSSA
EMI7 EMI6 AMI7 B7 EMI7 AMI7 B+7 B7
RHYTHM
mf
EMI7 AMI7 D7 GMA7
CMA7 AMI7 F#MI7 B7 F7
3
EMI7 AMI7 B+7 B7 EMI7
AMI7 D7 GMA7 CMA7 AMI7
F#MI7 B7 EMA7
3
3
F#MI7 B7 EMA7 AMI7
D7 GMA7 CMA7 AMI7 F#MI7

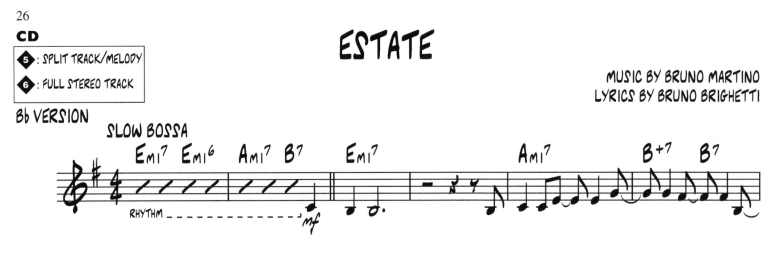

B7 F7 3 EMI7 AMI7
B+7 B7 EMI7 AMI7 D7
GMA7 CMA7 AMI7 F#MI7
B7 F7 3 EMI7 EMI6 AMI7 B7
EMI7 EMI6 3 CMA7 AMI7 F7 SOLO EMA7 F#MI7
B7 EMA7 AMI7 D7 GMA7 CMA7
AMI7 F#MI7 B7 F7 EMI7 AMI7
B+7 B7 EMI7 AMI7 D7 GMA7 CMA7
AMI7 F#MI7 B7 F7 3 EMI7 EMI6 AMI7
B7 EMI7 EMI6 AMI7 B7 EMI7

CD

7: SPLIT TRACK/MELODY

8: FULL STEREO TRACK

A FELICIDADE

WORDS AND MUSIC BY VINICIUS DE MORAES,
ANDRE SALVET AND ANTONIO CARLOS JOBIM

B♭ VERSION

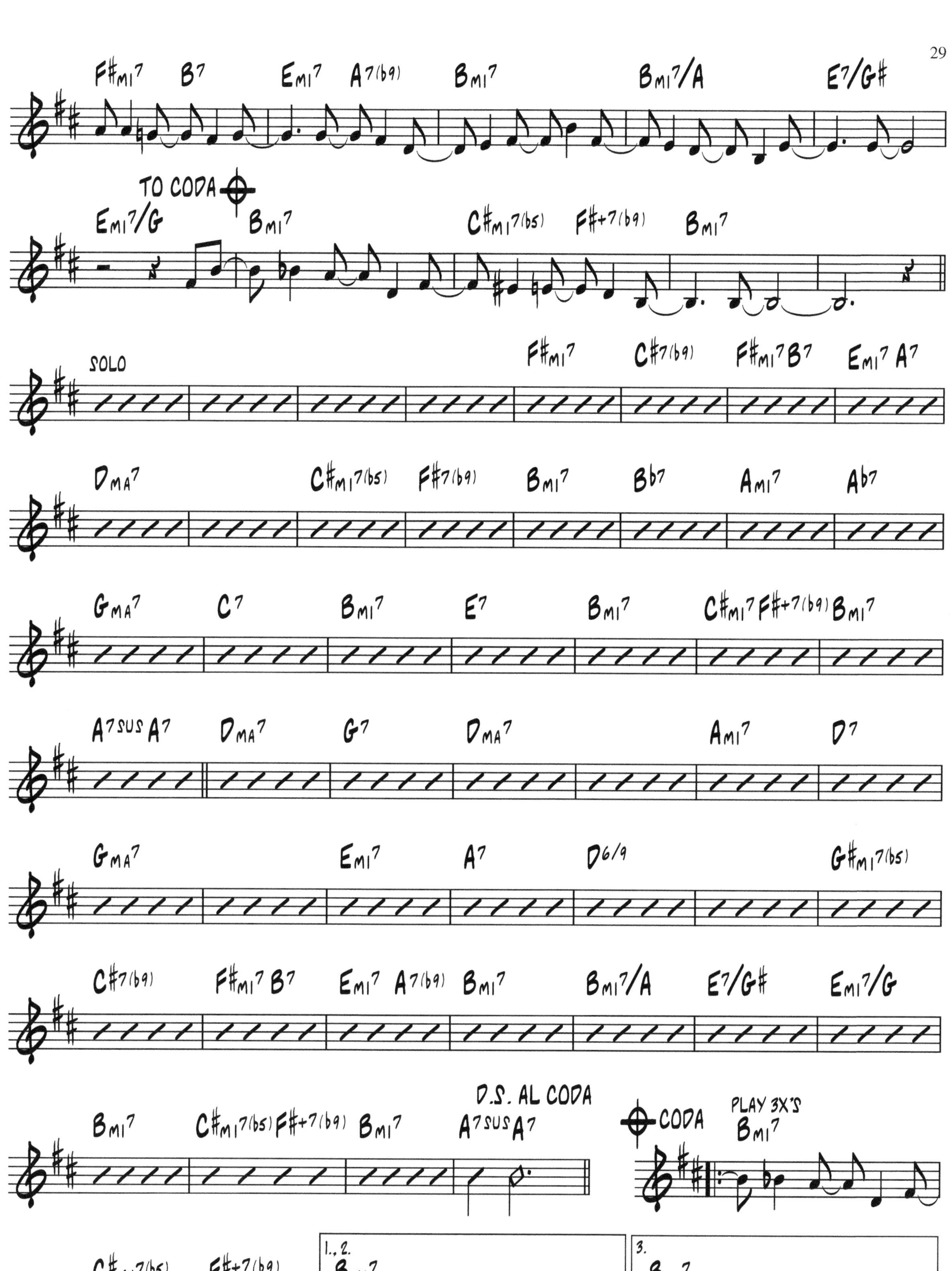
F♯MI7 B7 EMI7 A7(♭9) BMI7 BMI7/A E7/G♯
TO CODA
EMI7/G BMI7 C♯MI7(♭5) F♯+7(♭9) BMI7
SOLO
F♯MI7 C♯7(♭9) F♯MI7 B7 EMI7 A7
DMA7 C♯MI7(♭5) F♯7(♭9) BMI7 B♭7 AMI7 A♭7
GMA7 C7 BMI7 E7 BMI7 C♯MI7 F♯+7(♭9) BMI7
A7SUS A7 DMA7 G7 DMA7 AMI7 D7
GMA7 EMI7 A7 D6/9 G♯MI7(♭5)
C♯7(♭9) F♯MI7 B7 EMI7 A7(♭9) BMI7 BMI7/A E7/G♯ EMI7/G
D.S. AL CODA
BMI7 C♯MI7(♭5) F♯+7(♭9) BMI7 A7SUS A7
CODA
PLAY 3X'S
BMI7
C♯MI7(♭5) F♯+7(♭9)
1., 2.
BMI7
3.
BMI7

CD
9 : SPLIT TRACK/MELODY
10 : FULL STEREO TRACK

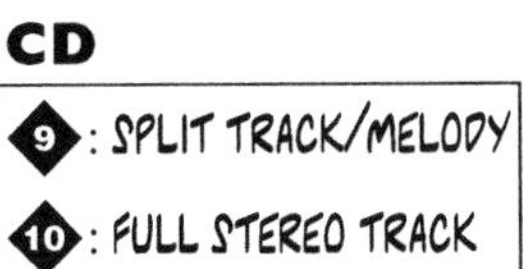

FLAMINGO

LYRIC BY ED ANDERSON
MUSIC BY TED GROUYA

Bb VERSION

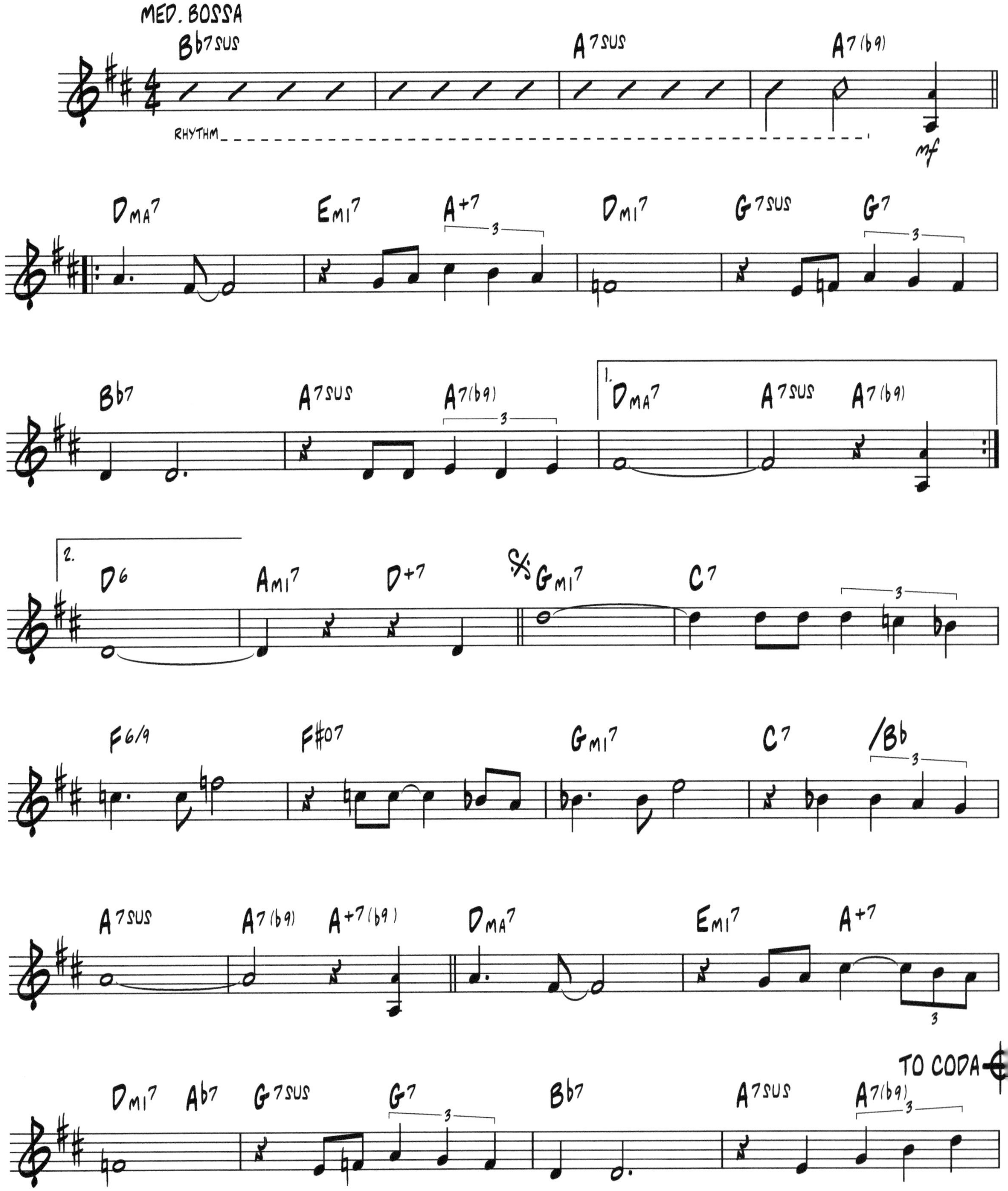

MED. BOSSA
Bb7SUS
A7SUS
A7(b9)
RHYTHM
mf
DMA7
EMI7
A+7
DMI7
G7SUS
G7
Bb7
A7SUS
A7(b9)
1.
DMA7
A7SUS
A7(b9)
2.
D6
AMI7
D+7
GMI7
C7
F6/9
F#07
GMI7
C7
/Bb
A7SUS
A7(b9)
A+7(b9)
DMA7
EMI7
A+7
TO CODA
DMI7
Ab7
G7SUS
G7
Bb7
A7SUS
A7(b9)

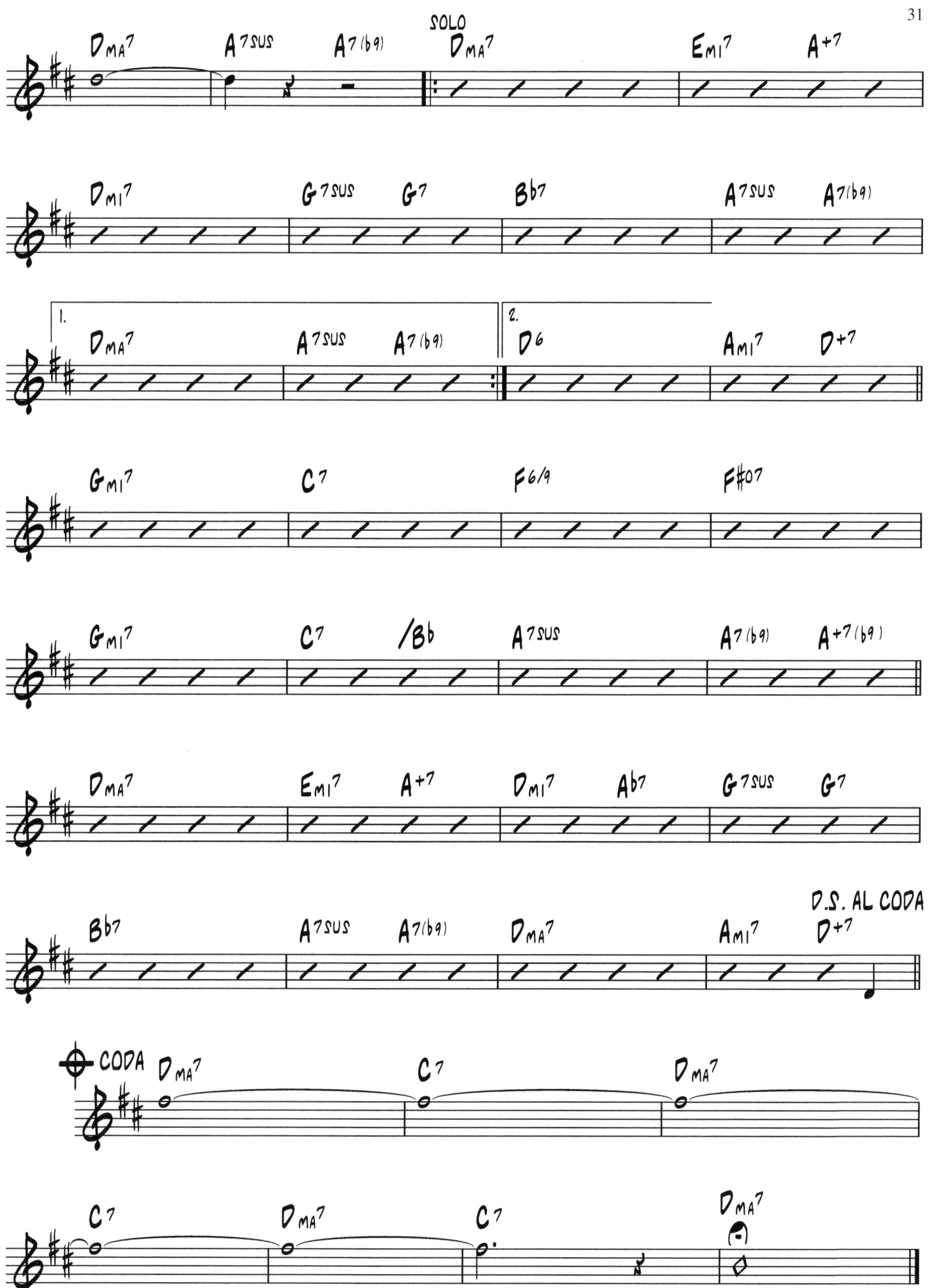

SOLO
DMA7
A7SUS
A7(b9)
DMA7
EMI7
A+7
DMI7
G7SUS
G7
Bb7
A7SUS
A7(b9)
1.
DMA7
A7SUS
A7(b9)
2.
D6
AMI7
D+7
GMI7
C7
F6/9
F#o7
GMI7
C7
/Bb
A7SUS
A7(b9)
A+7(b9)
DMA7
EMI7
A+7
DMI7
Ab7
G7SUS
G7
Bb7
A7SUS
A7(b9)
DMA7
AMI7
D+7
D.S. AL CODA
CODA
DMA7
C7
DMA7
C7
DMA7
C7
DMA7

CD

11: SPLIT TRACK/MELODY
12: FULL STEREO TRACK

WORDS AND MUSIC BY
ALBERTO DOMINGUEZ

Bb VERSION

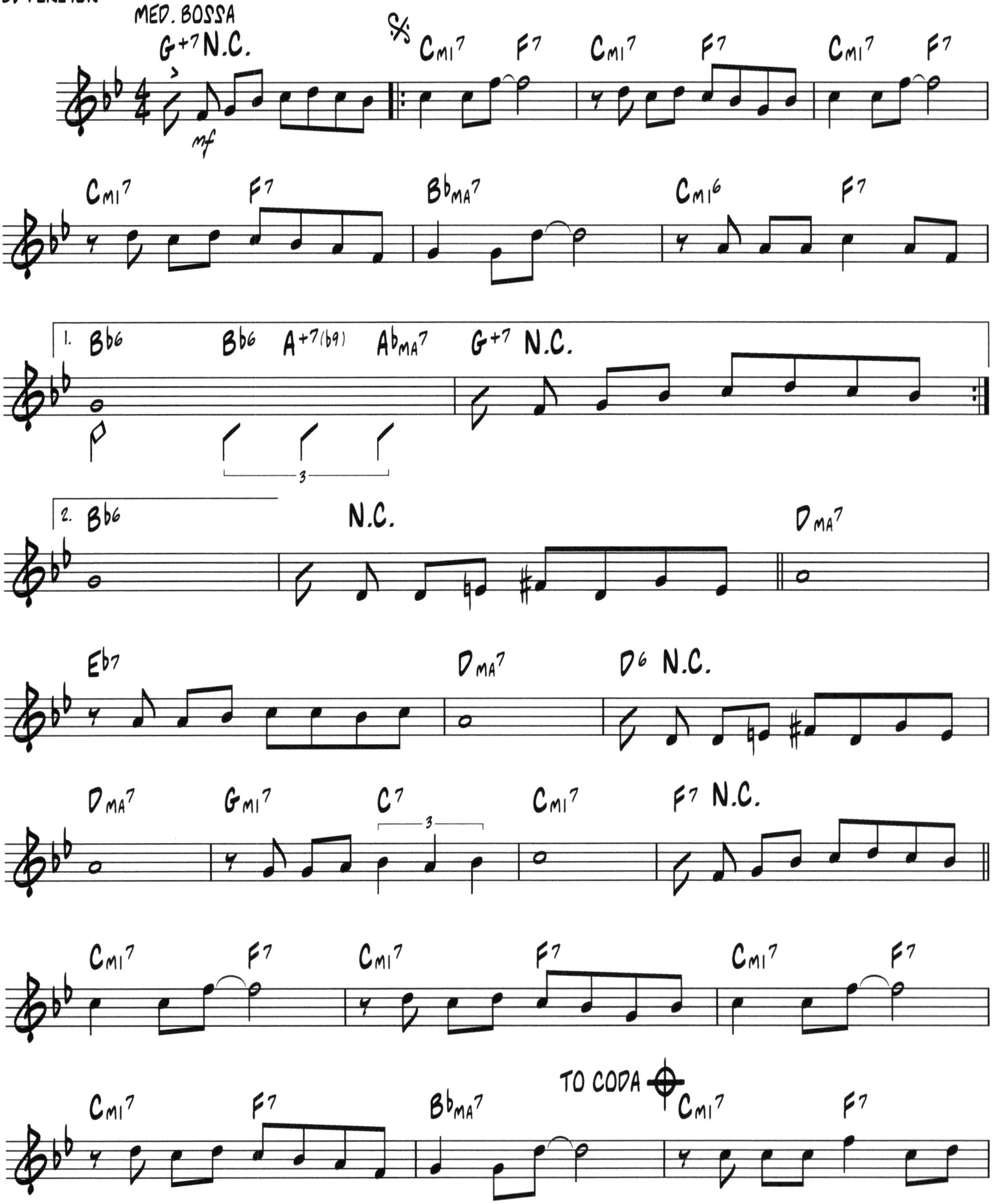

MED. BOSSA

G+7 N.C. | Cmi7 F7 | Cmi7 F7 | Cmi7 F7

Cmi7 F7 | Bbma7 | Cmi6 F7

1. Bb6 Bb6 A+7(b9) Abma7 | G+7 N.C.

2. Bb6 | N.C. | Dma7

Eb7 | Dma7 | D6 N.C.

Dma7 | Gmi7 C7 | Cmi7 | F7 N.C.

Cmi7 F7 | Cmi7 F7 | Cmi7 F7

Cmi7 F7 | Bbma7 | TO CODA Cmi7 F7

Bb6
Bb6 A+7(b9) Abma7
G+7
SOLO BREAK
SOLO
Cmi7
F7
Cmi7 F7 Cmi7 F7 Cmi7 F7
Bbma7 Cmi6 F7
1. Bb6 Bb6 A+7(b9) Abma7
3
G+7
2. Bb6
Dma7 Eb7 Dma7 D6
Dma7 Gmi7 C7 Cmi7 F7
Cmi7 F7 Cmi7 F7 Cmi7 F7 Cmi7 F7 Bbma7
Cmi7 F7 Bb6 Bb6 A+7(b9) Abma7 G+7 N.C.
D.S. AL CODA
TAKE REPEAT
CODA
Cmi7
B9(#11)
Bbma7

CD

13: SPLIT TRACK/MELODY
14: FULL STEREO TRACK

HO-BA-LA-LA

WORDS AND MUSIC BY NORMAN GIMBEL
AND JOAO GILBERTO

Bb VERSION

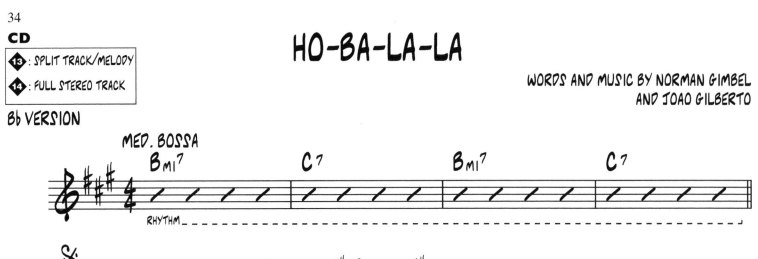

TO CODA
Bmi7 E7 A6 C#mi7(b5) F#+7(b9)
SOLO
Bmi7 E7 E#o7 F#mi7
C7 Bmi7 E7
1. C#mi7(b5) F#+7(b9)
2. A6 Eb7
Dmi7 G7 Cma7 C#o7
Dmi7 G7 Bmi7 E7 C#mi7(b5) F#+7(b9)
Bmi7 E7 E#o7 F#mi7 C7
Bmi7 E7 A6 C7 D.S. AL CODA
CODA
Dma7 C7 Dma7 C7
Dma7 C7 Dma7 C7 Ama7
RIT.

CD

15: SPLIT TRACK/MELODY

16: FULL STEREO TRACK

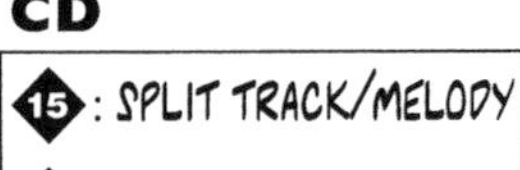

MENINA FLOR

WORDS BY MARIA TOLEDO
MUSIC BY LUIZ BONFA

Bb VERSION

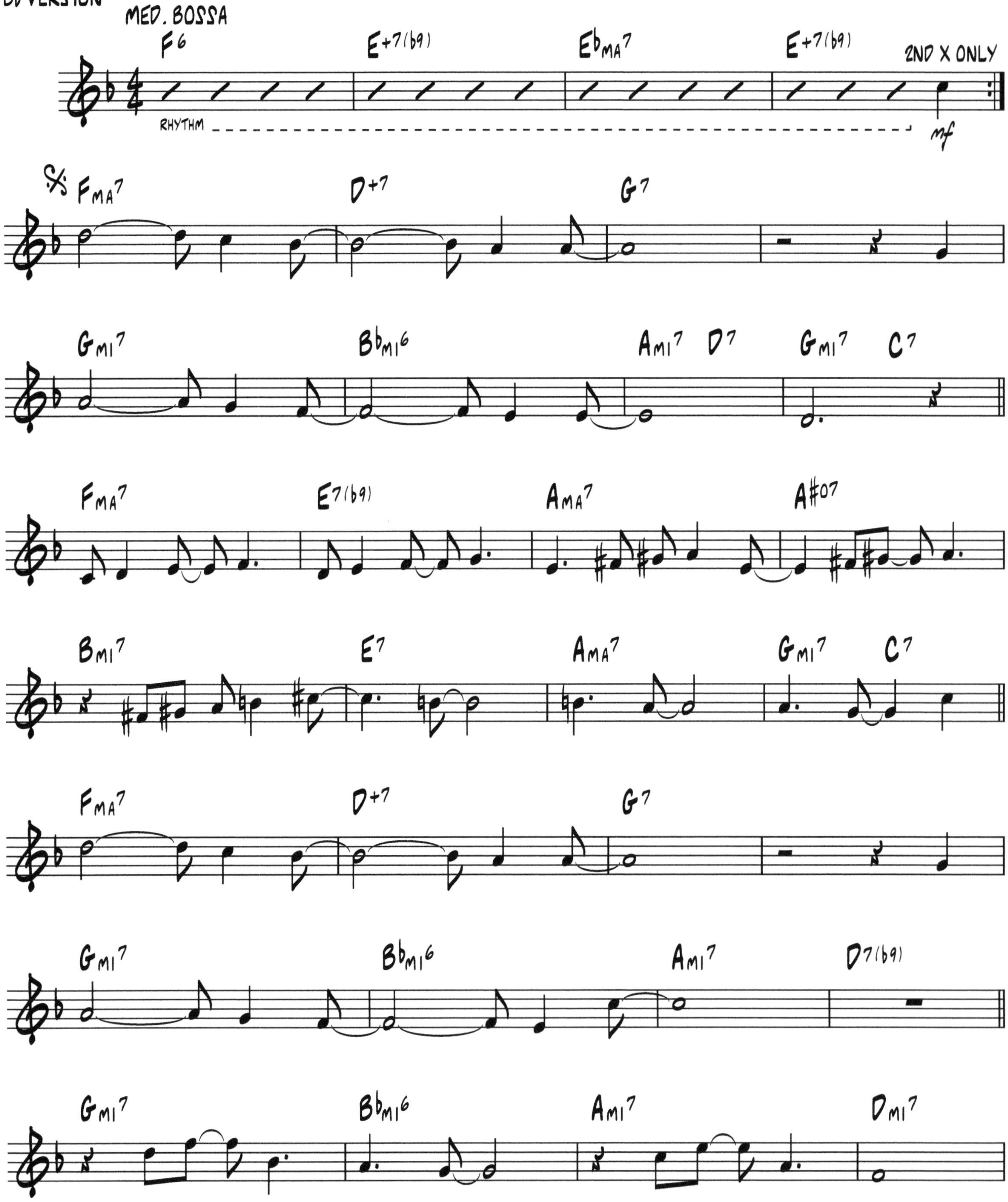

MED. BOSSA
F6
E+7(b9)
EbMA7
E+7(b9)
2ND X ONLY
RHYTHM
mf
FMA7
D+7
G7
GMI7
BbMI6
AMI7
D7
GMI7
C7
FMA7
E7(b9)
AMA7
A#o7
BMI7
E7
AMA7
GMI7
C7
FMA7
D+7
G7
GMI7
BbMI6
AMI7
D7(b9)
GMI7
BbMI6
AMI7
DMI7

TO CODA
GMI7
C7SUS
C7
F6
GMI7 C7
SOLOS (2 CHORUSES)
FMA7
D+7
G7
GMI7
B♭MI6
AMI7 D7
GMI7 C7
FMA7
E7(♭9)
AMA7
A♯o7
BMI7
E7
AMA7
GMI7 C7
FMA7
D+7
G7
GMI7
B♭MI6
AMI7
D7(♭9)
GMI7
B♭MI6
AMI7
DMI7
D.S. AL CODA
GMI7
C7SUS
C7
F6
GMI7 C7
2ND X ONLY
CODA
F6
E+7(♭9)
E♭MA7
E+7(♭9)
F6
E+7(♭9)
E♭MA7
E+7(♭9)
F6

CD

17: SPLIT TRACK/MELODY
18: FULL STEREO TRACK

Bb VERSION

O PATO
(THE DUCK)

WORDS AND MUSIC BY JAYME SILVA AND NEUZA TEIXIERA
ENGLISH LYRIC BY JON HENDRICKS

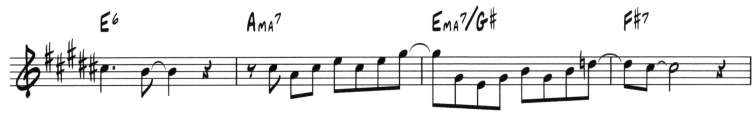

B7 EMA7 F♯7

TO CODA F7 E6 SOLO BREAK

SOLOS (2 FULL CHORUSES)

E6 F♯7 F♯MI7 B7

E6 BMI7 E7 AMA7

F♯7 B7SUS EMA7 BMI7 E7

AMA7 D7 E6 AMA7 D7 E6

AMA7 EMA7/G♯ F♯7 B7 EMA7

F♯7 F7(♯9) E6 D.S. AL CODA

CODA F7 C+7 B7(♭9) E6

CD

19 : SPLIT TRACK/MELODY
20 : FULL STEREO TRACK

PETITE FLEUR
(LITTLE FLOWER)

BY SIDNEY BECHET

TO CODA
BMI7(b5) F7 E7(b9) AMI7 E+7(b9)
SOLO
BMI7(b5) E7(b9) AMI7 D7 F#MI7(b5) B7(b9)
BMI7(b5) E+7(b9) BMI7(b5) E7(b9) CMA7 C#o7
DMI7 G7 CMA7 C6 BMI7(b5) E7(b9)
AMI7 D7 F#MI7(b5) B7(b9) BMI7(b5) E+7(b9)
BMI7(b5) E7(b9) AMI7 D7
BMI7(b5) F7 E7(b9) AMI7 E+7(b9)
D.S. AL CODA
CODA
AMI7 D7 GMA7
FMA7 BMI7(b5) BMI7(b5)/E AMI7

CD

3 : SPLIT TRACK/MELODY
4 : FULL STEREO TRACK

BOSSA ANTIGUA

BY PAUL DESMOND

Eb VERSION

GMI7
C7
AMI7
DMI7
GMI7
C7
FMA7
D+7
TO CODA
SOLO
GMI7
C7
AMI7
DMI7
GMI7
1.
C7
AMI7
D7
2.
BMI7
E7
AMA7
F#MI7
BMI7
E7
C#MI7
F#MI7
BMI7
E7
AMI7
D7
GMI7
C7
AMI7
DMI7
D.S. AL CODA
GMI7
C7
FMA7
GMI7
C7
CODA
GMI7
C7
GMI7
C7
AMI7
D+7
AMI7
D+7
GMI7
C7
GMI7
C7
FMA7

CD

5 : SPLIT TRACK/MELODY
6 : FULL STEREO TRACK

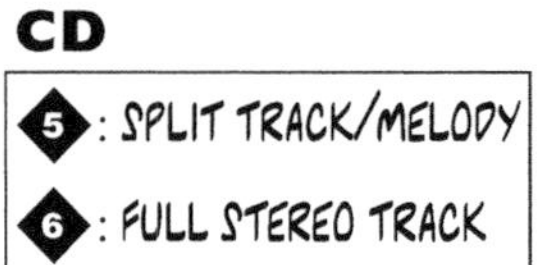

ESTATE

MUSIC BY BRUNO MARTINO
LYRICS BY BRUNO BRIGHETTI

E♭ VERSION

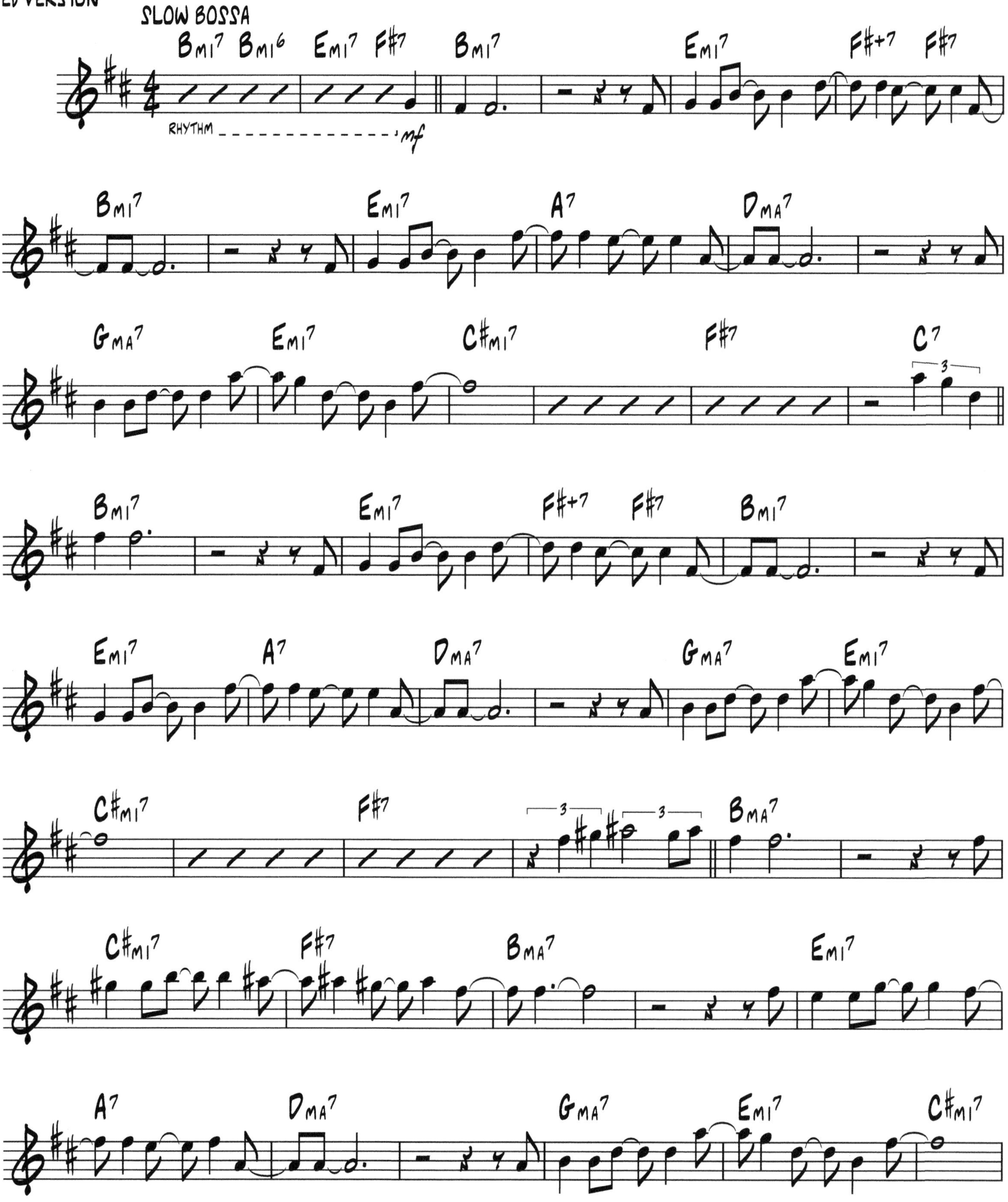

SLOW BOSSA
BMI7 BMI6 EMI7 F#7 BMI7 EMI7 F#+7 F#7
RHYTHM
mf
BMI7 EMI7 A7 DMA7
GMA7 EMI7 C#MI7 F#7 C7
3
BMI7 EMI7 F#+7 F#7 BMI7
EMI7 A7 DMA7 GMA7 EMI7
C#MI7 F#7 BMA7
3
3
C#MI7 F#7 BMA7 EMI7
A7 DMA7 GMA7 EMI7 C#MI7

F#7 C7 Bmi7 Emi7
F#+7 F#7 Bmi7 Emi7 A7
Dma7 Gma7 Emi7 C#mi7
F#7 C7 Bmi7 Bmi6 Emi7 F#7
Bmi7 Bmi6 Gma7 Emi7 C7 SOLO Bma7 C#mi7
F#7 Bma7 Emi7 A7 Dma7 Gma7
Emi7 C#mi7 F#7 C7 Bmi7 Emi7
F#+7 F#7 Bmi7 Emi7 A7 Dma7 Gma7
Emi7 C#mi7 F#7 C7 Bmi7 Bmi6 Emi7
F#7 Bmi7 Bmi6 Emi7 F#7 Bmi7

CD

A FELICIDADE

WORDS AND MUSIC BY VINICIUS DE MORAES,
ANDRE SALVET AND ANTONIO CARLOS JOBIM

E♭ VERSION

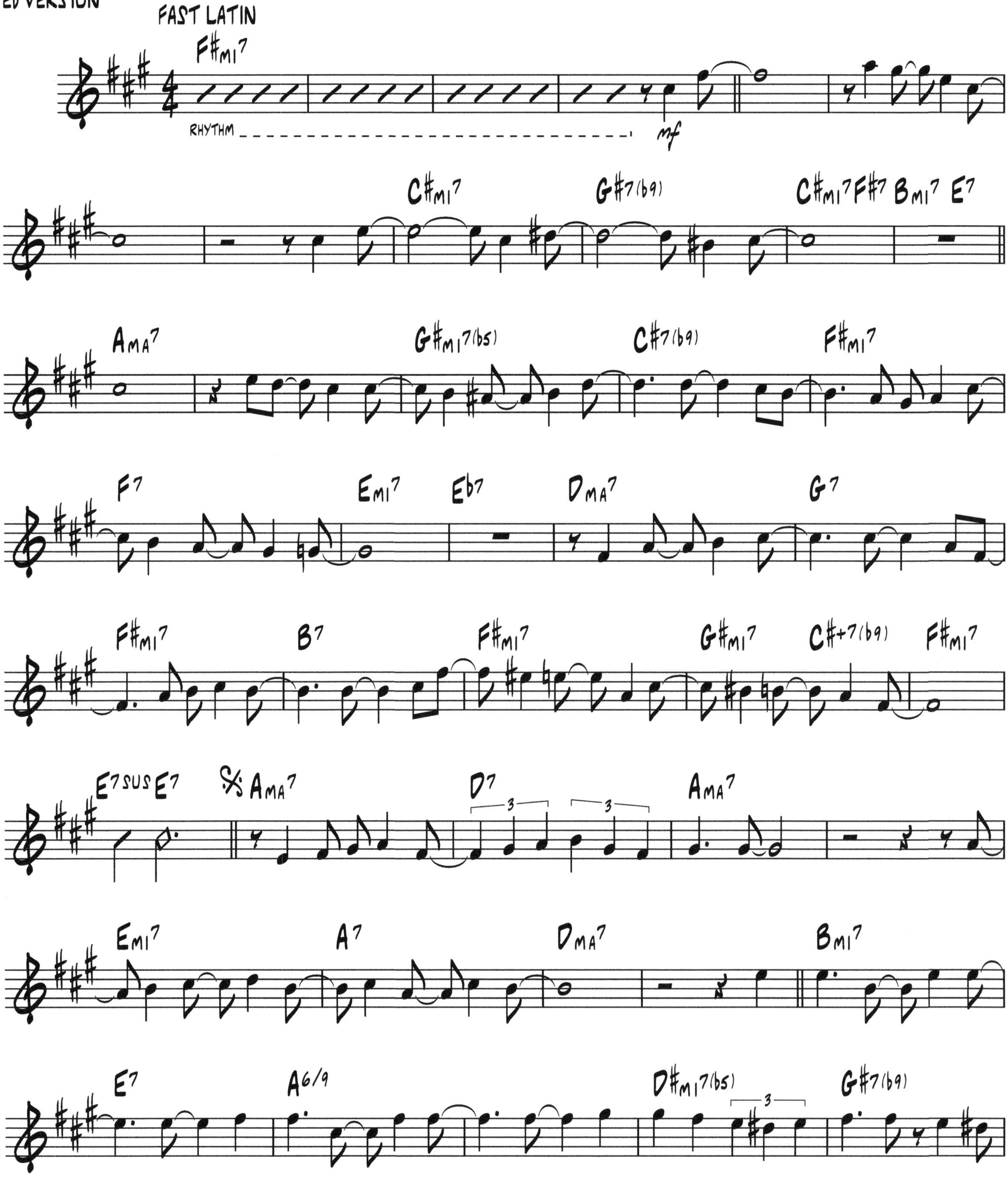

FAST LATIN

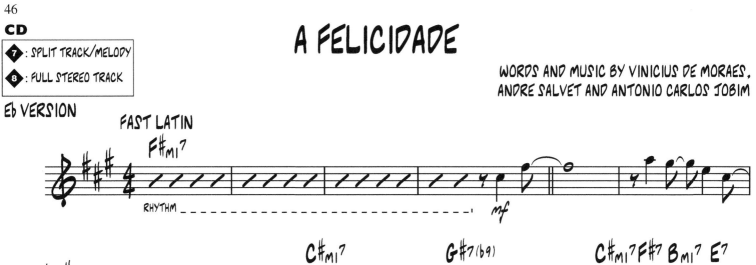

C#mi7 F#7 Bmi7 E7(b9) F#mi7 F#mi7/E B7/D#
TO CODA
Bmi7/D F#mi7 G#mi7(b5) C#+7(b9) F#mi7
SOLO
C#mi7 G#7(b9) C#mi7 F#7 Bmi7 E7
Ama7 G#mi7(b5) C#7(b9) F#mi7 F7 Emi7 Eb7
Dma7 G7 F#mi7 B7 F#mi7 G#mi7 C#+7(b9) F#mi7
E7sus E7 Ama7 D7 Ama7 Emi7 A7
Dma7 Bmi7 E7 A6/9 D#mi7(b5)
G#7(b9) C#mi7 F#7 Bmi7 E7(b9) F#mi7 F#mi7/E B7/D# Bmi7/D
D.S. AL CODA
F#mi7 G#mi7(b5) C#+7(b9) F#mi7 E7sus E7
CODA
PLAY 3X'S
F#mi7
G#mi7(b5) C#+7(b9)
1., 2.
F#mi7
3.
F#mi7

CD

FLAMINGO

LYRIC BY ED ANDERSON
MUSIC BY TED GROUYA

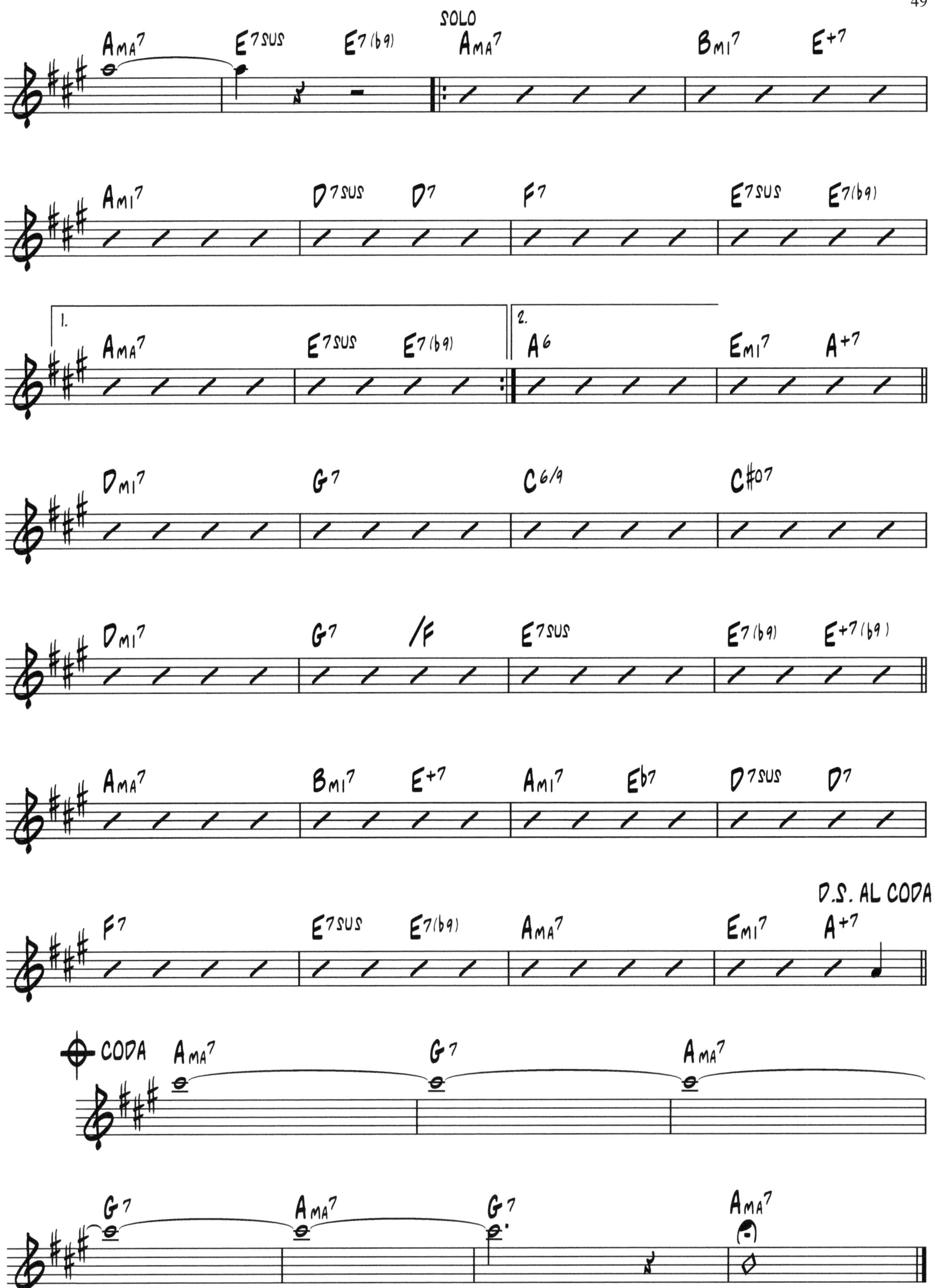

SOLO
AMA7 E7SUS E7(b9) AMA7 BMI7 E+7
AMI7 D7SUS D7 F7 E7SUS E7(b9)
1. AMA7 E7SUS E7(b9)
2. A6 EMI7 A+7
DMI7 G7 C6/9 C#07
DMI7 G7 /F E7SUS E7(b9) E+7(b9)
AMA7 BMI7 E+7 AMI7 Eb7 D7SUS D7
D.S. AL CODA
F7 E7SUS E7(b9) AMA7 EMI7 A+7
CODA AMA7 G7 AMA7
G7 AMA7 G7 AMA7

CD

11: SPLIT TRACK/MELODY

12: FULL STEREO TRACK

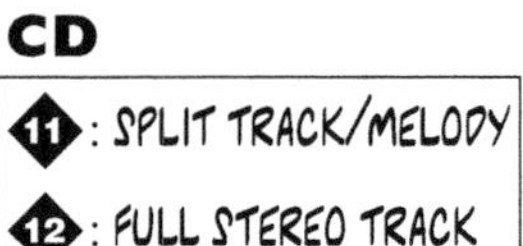

FRENESÍ

WORDS AND MUSIC BY
ALBERTO DOMINGUEZ

Eb VERSION

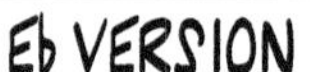

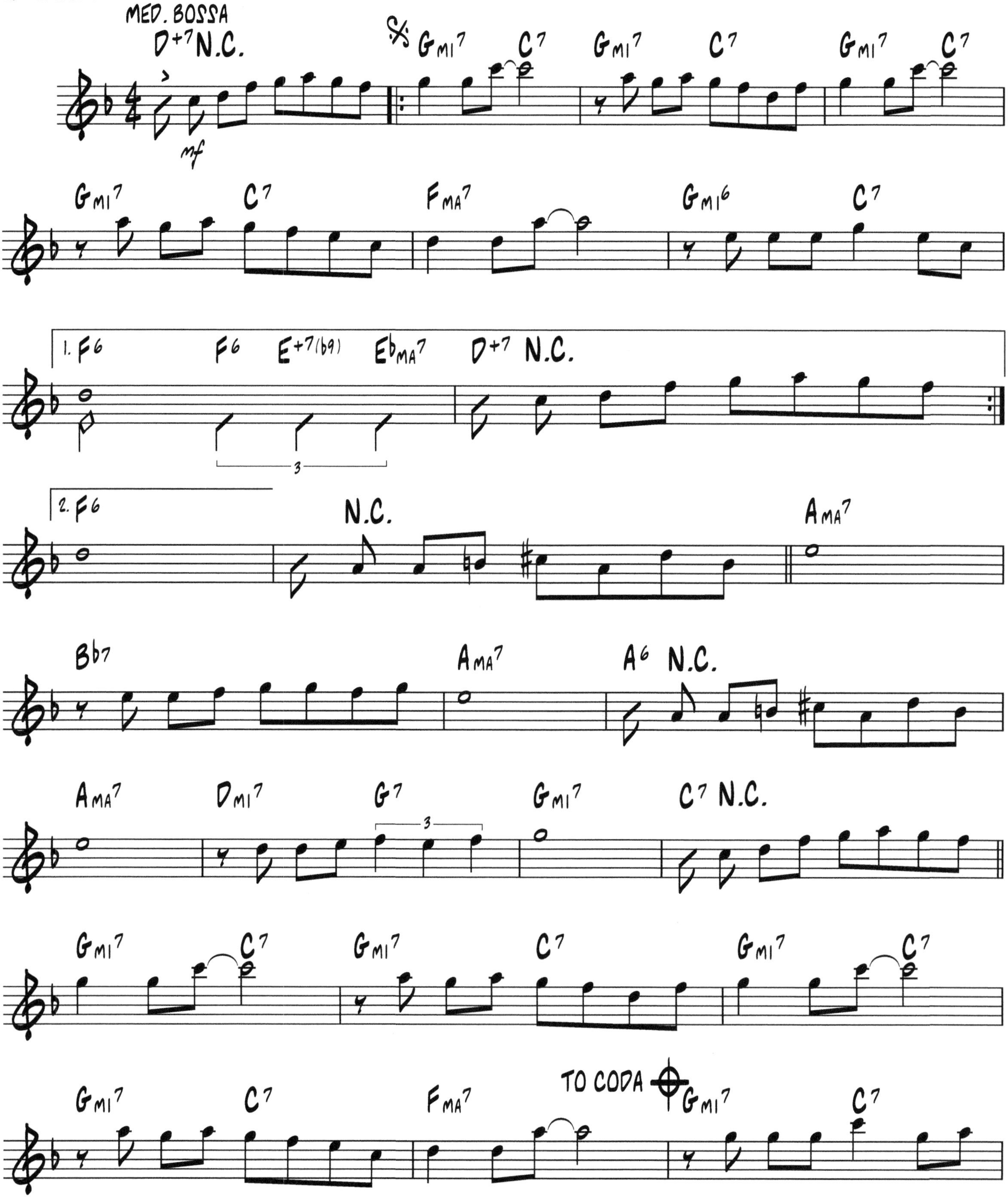

MED. BOSSA
D+7 N.C.
GMI7 C7 GMI7 C7 GMI7 C7
mf
GMI7 C7 FMA7 GMI6 C7
1. F6 F6 E+7(b9) EbMA7 D+7 N.C.
3
2. F6 N.C. AMA7
Bb7 AMA7 A6 N.C.
AMA7 DMI7 G7 GMI7 C7 N.C.
3
GMI7 C7 GMI7 C7 GMI7 C7
GMI7 C7 FMA7 TO CODA GMI7 C7

F6
F6 E+7(b9) Ebma7
D+7
SOLO BREAK
SOLO
Gmi7
C7
Fma7
Gmi6
1.
2.
D+7
F6
Ama7
Bb7
A6
Dmi7
G7
N.C.
D.S. AL CODA
TAKE REPEAT
CODA
F#9(#11)

CD

HO-BA-LA-LA

WORDS AND MUSIC BY NORMAN GIMBEL
AND JOAO GILBERTO

Eb VERSION

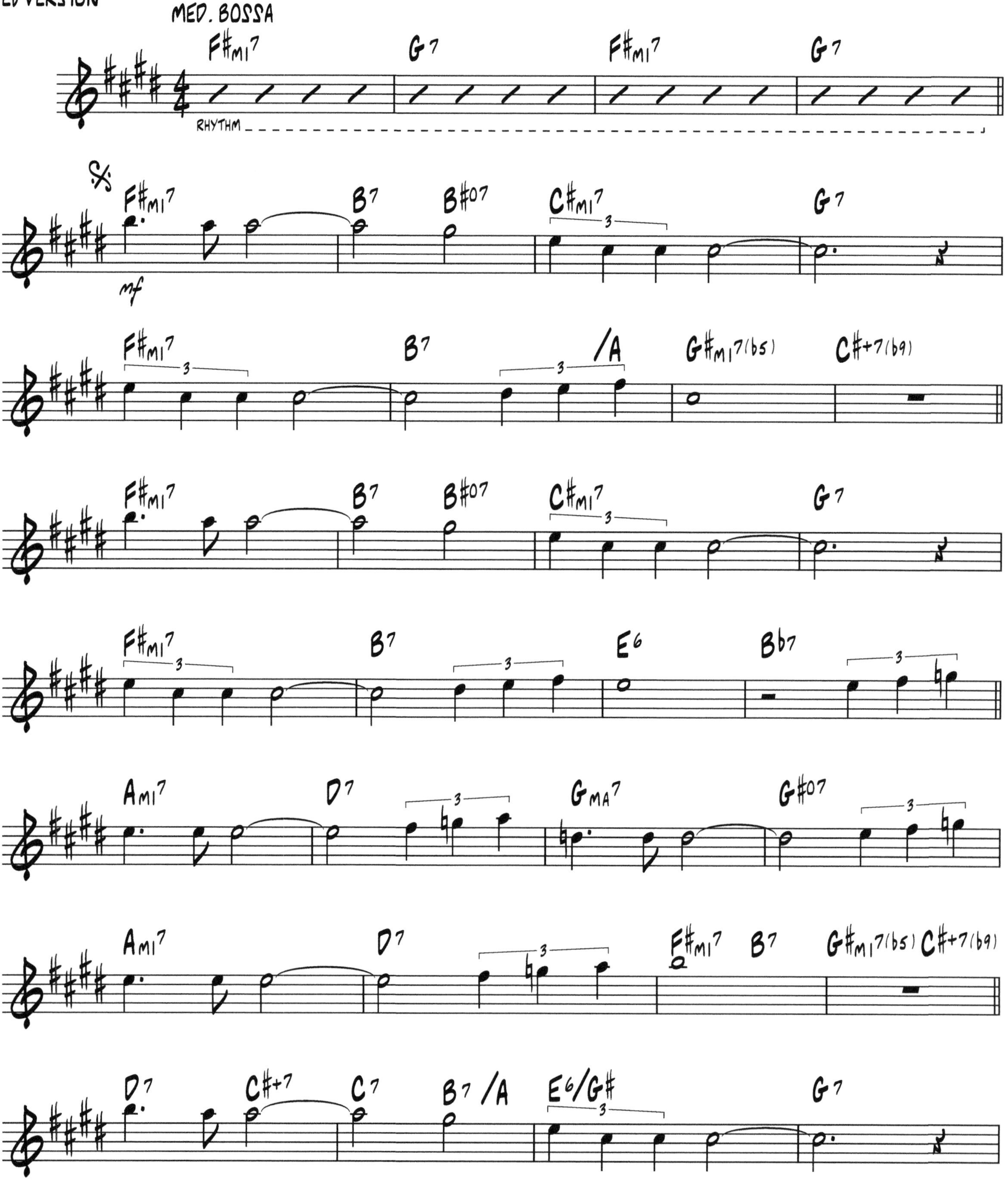

MED. BOSSA

F#MI7 G7 F#MI7 G7

RHYTHM

F#MI7 B7 B#o7 C#MI7 G7

mf

F#MI7 B7 /A G#MI7(b5) C#+7(b9)

F#MI7 B7 B#o7 C#MI7 G7

F#MI7 B7 E6 Bb7

AMI7 D7 GMA7 G#o7

AMI7 D7 F#MI7 B7 G#MI7(b5) C#+7(b9)

D7 C#+7 C7 B7 /A E6/G# G7

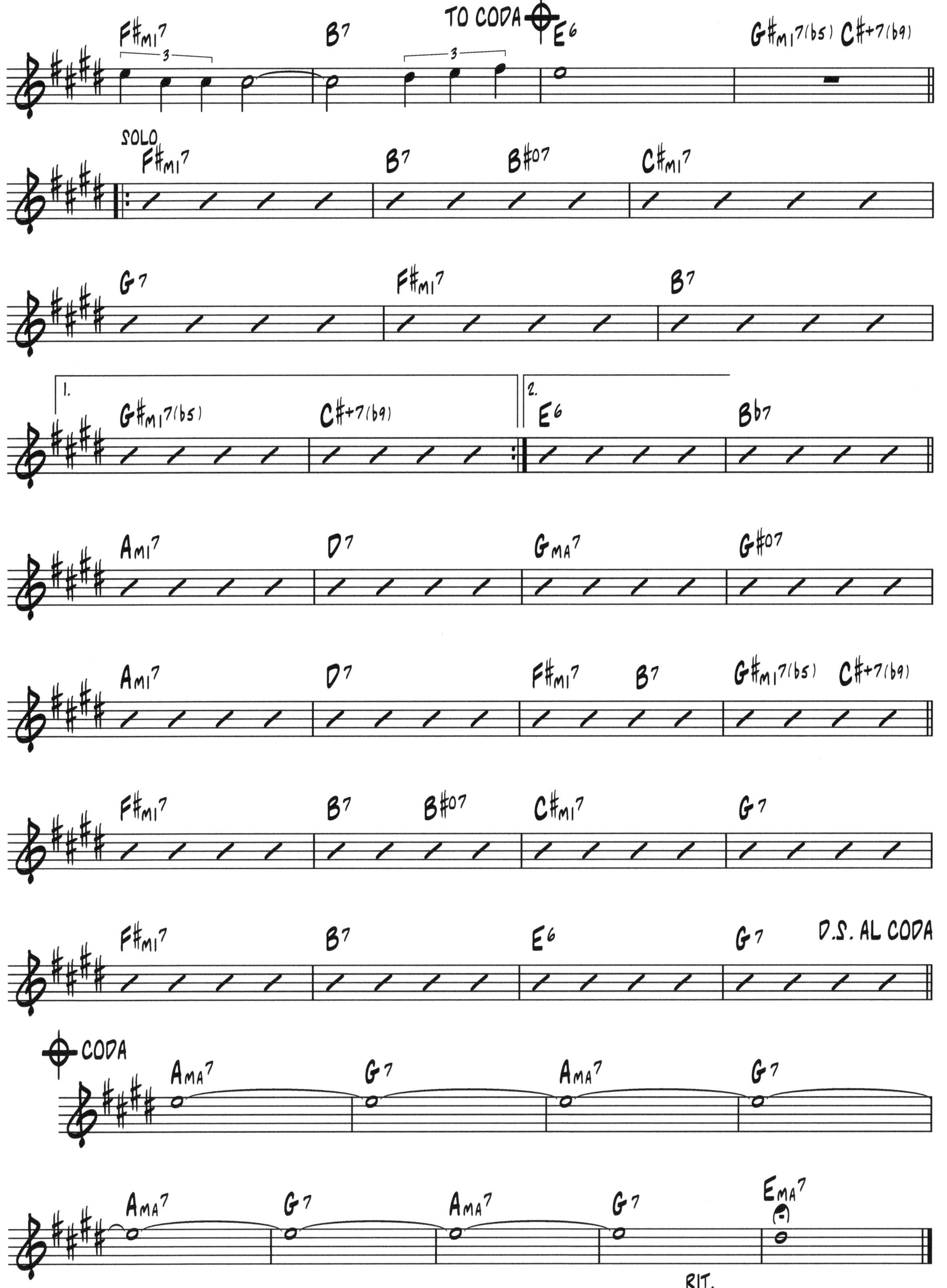

TO CODA
F♯MI7
B7
E6
G♯MI7(b5)
C♯+7(b9)
SOLO
F♯MI7
B7
B♯07
C♯MI7
G7
F♯MI7
B7
1.
G♯MI7(b5)
C♯+7(b9)
2.
E6
Bb7
AMI7
D7
GMA7
G♯07
AMI7
D7
F♯MI7
B7
G♯MI7(b5)
C♯+7(b9)
F♯MI7
B7
B♯07
C♯MI7
G7
F♯MI7
B7
E6
G7
D.S. AL CODA
CODA
AMA7
G7
AMA7
G7
AMA7
G7
AMA7
G7
EMA7
RIT.

CD

15: SPLIT TRACK/MELODY

16: FULL STEREO TRACK

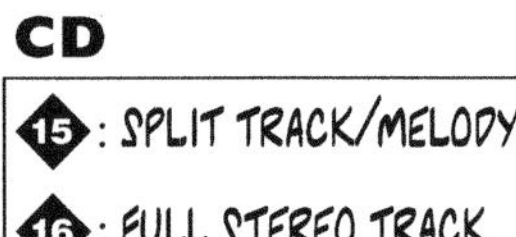

MENINA FLOR

WORDS BY MARIA TOLEDO
MUSIC BY LUIZ BONFA

Eb VERSION

MED. BOSSA
C6 B+7(b9) Bbma7 B+7(b9) 2ND X ONLY
RHYTHM
mf
Cma7 A+7 D7
Dmi7 Fmi6 Emi7 A7 Dmi7 G7
Cma7 B7(b9) Ema7 E#o7
F#mi7 B7 Ema7 Dmi7 G7
Cma7 A+7 D7
Dmi7 Fmi6 Emi7 A7(b9)
Dmi7 Fmi6 Emi7 Ami7

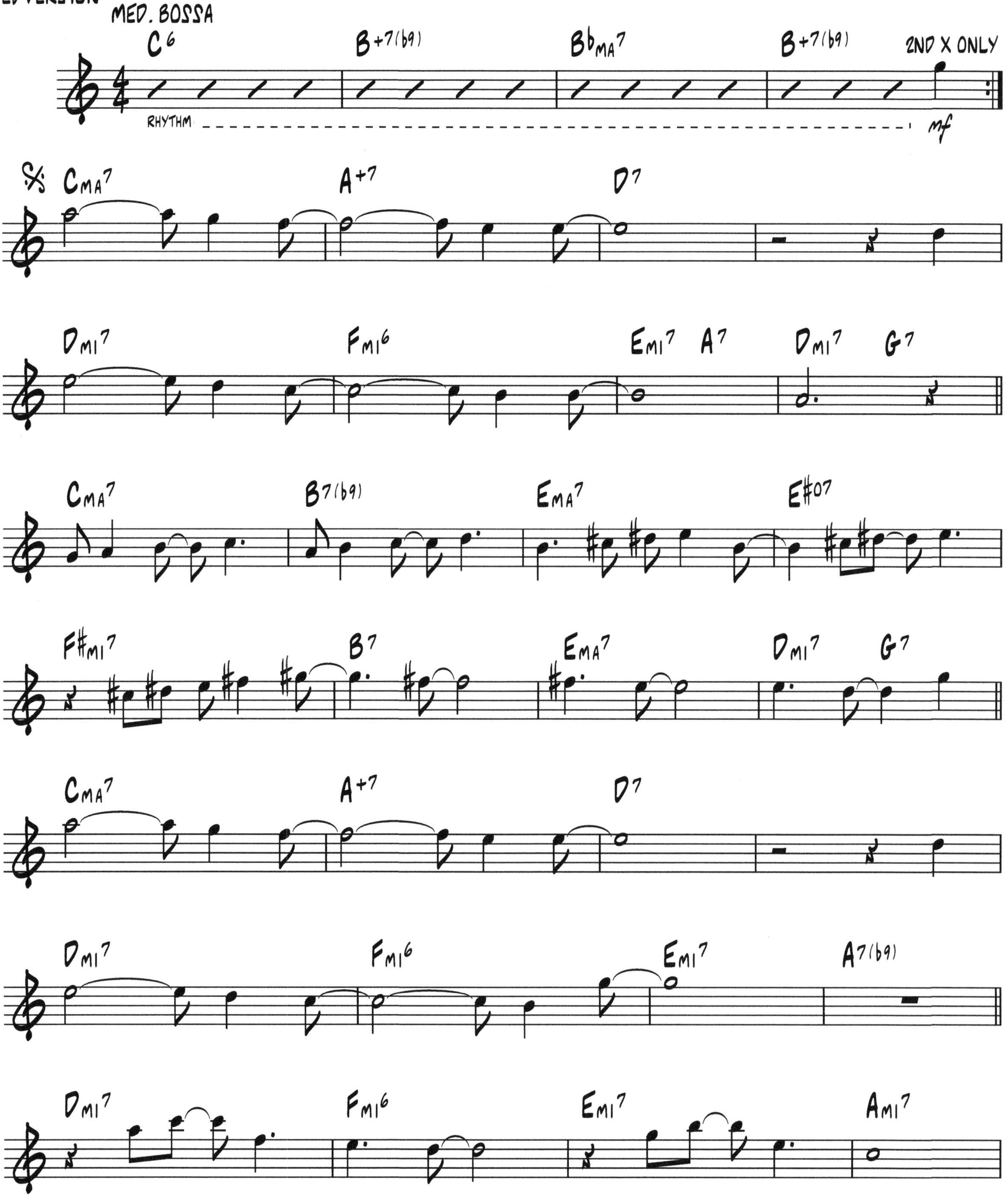

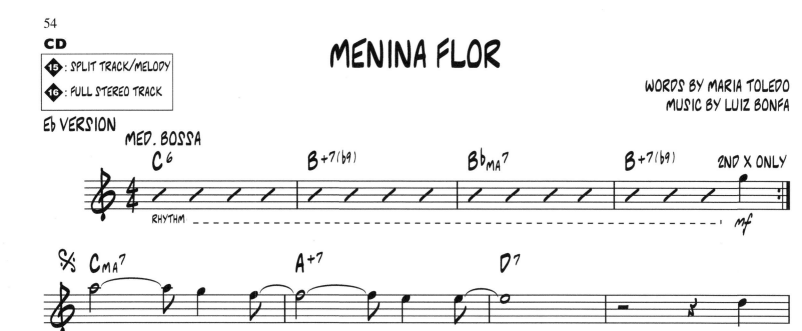

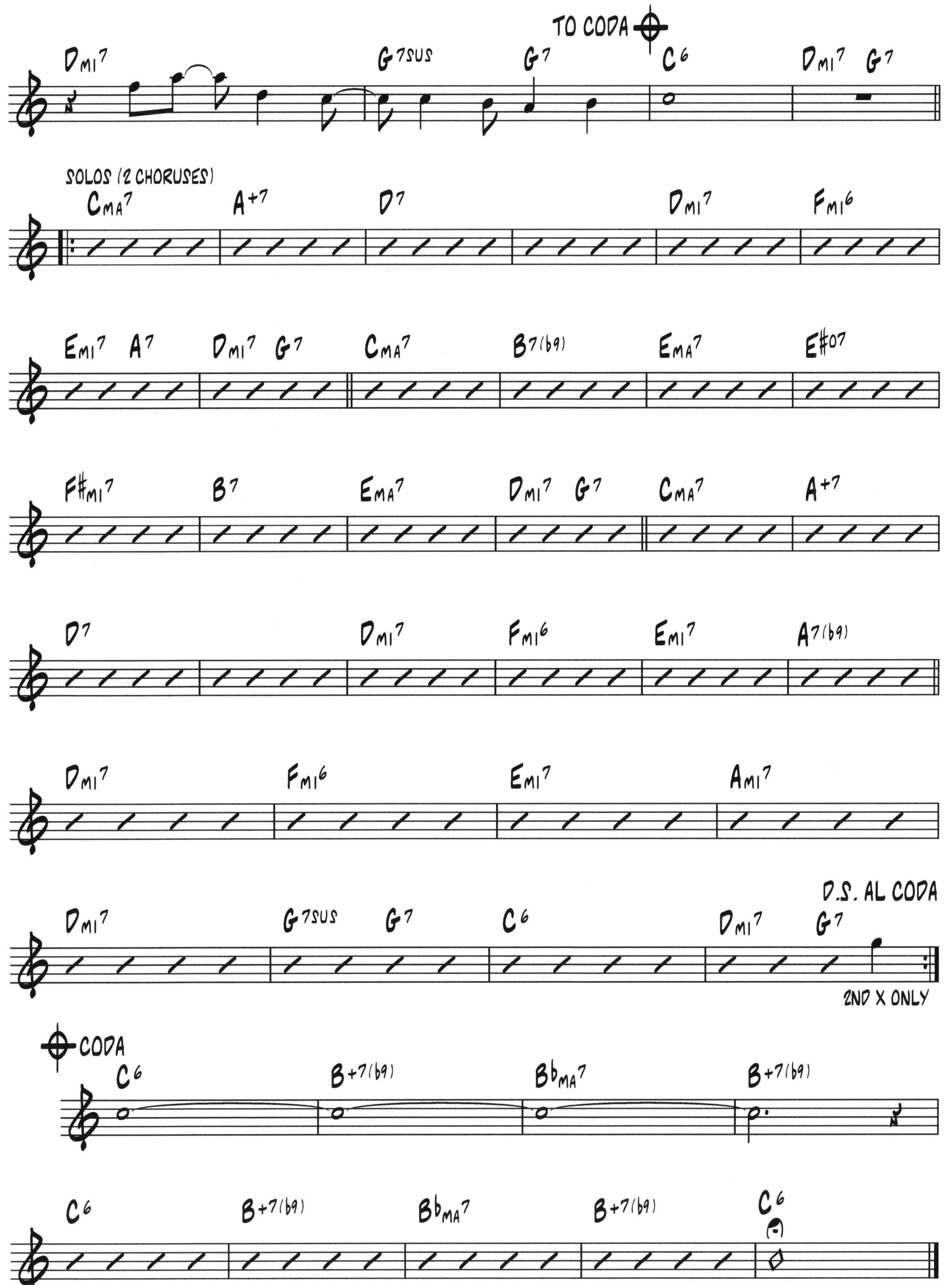
TO CODA
SOLOS (2 CHORUSES)
D.S. AL CODA
2ND X ONLY
CODA

CD

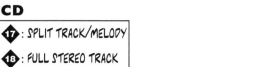

17: SPLIT TRACK/MELODY
18: FULL STEREO TRACK

O PATO
(THE DUCK)

WORDS AND MUSIC BY JAYME SILVA AND NEUZA TEIXIERA
ENGLISH LYRIC BY JON HENDRICKS

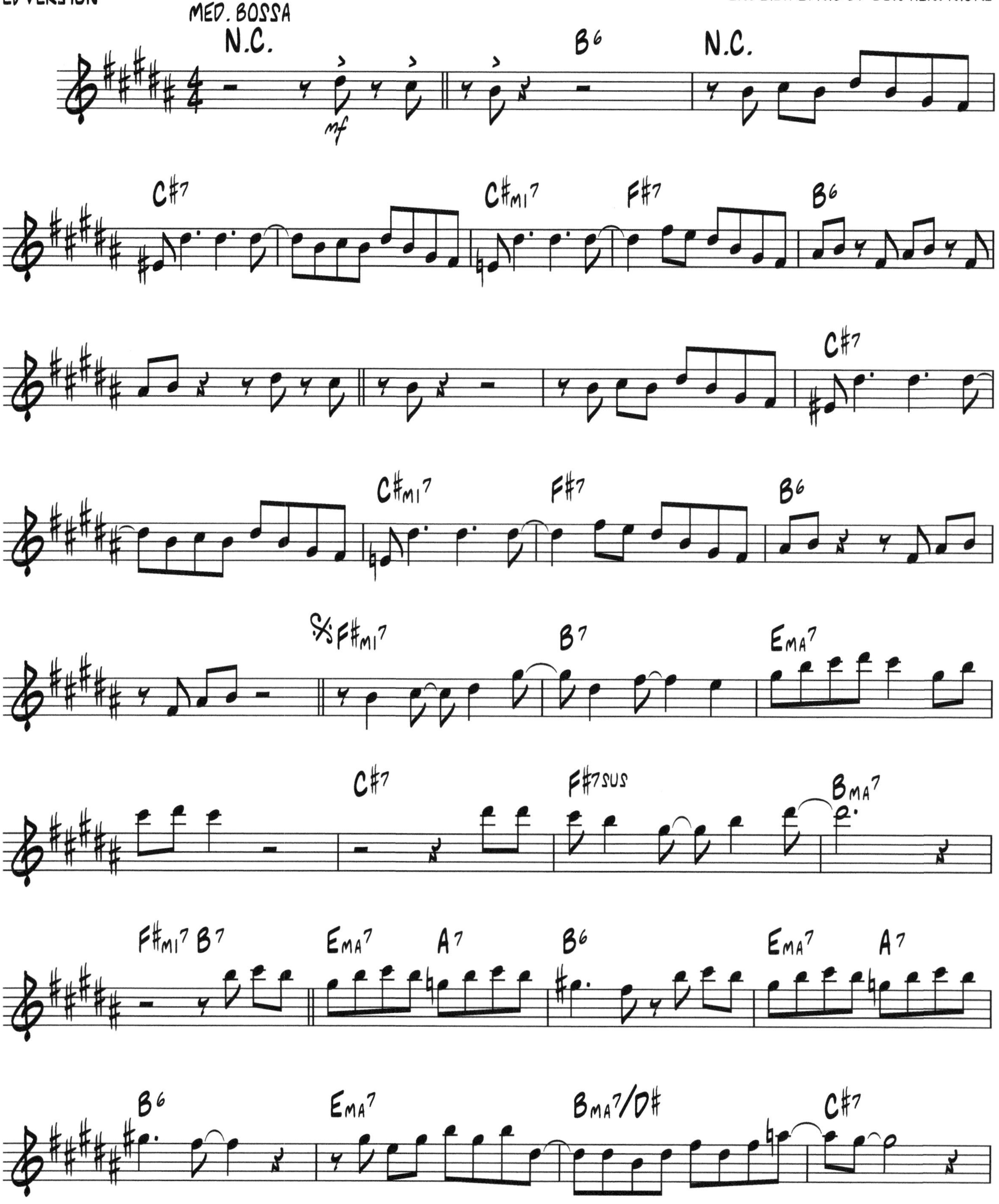

E♭ VERSION

MED. BOSSA
N.C.
mf
B6
N.C.
C♯7
C♯MI7
F♯7
B6
C♯7
C♯MI7
F♯7
B6
F♯MI7
B7
EMA7
C♯7
F♯7SUS
BMA7
F♯MI7 B7
EMA7
A7
B6
EMA7
A7
B6
EMA7
BMA7/D♯
C♯7

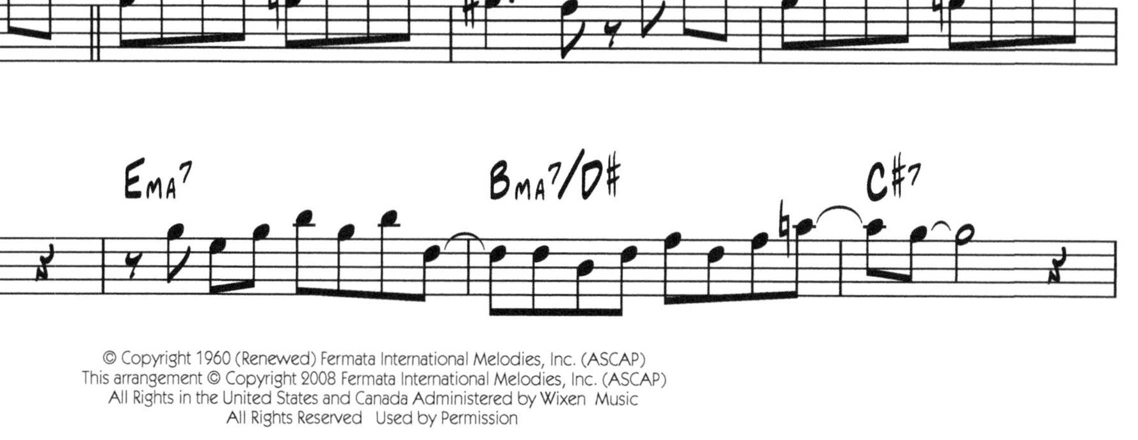

F♯7
BMA7
C♯7
TO CODA
C7
B6
SOLO BREAK
SOLOS (2 FULL CHORUSES)
B6
C♯7
C♯MI7
F♯7
B6
F♯MI7
B7
EMA7
C♯7
F♯7SUS
BMA7
F♯MI7
B7
EMA7
A7
B6
EMA7
A7
B6
EMA7
BMA7/D♯
C♯7
F♯7
BMA7
C♯7
C7(♯9)
B6
D.S. AL CODA
CODA
C7
G+7
F♯7(♭9)
B6

CD

19: SPLIT TRACK/MELODY
20: FULL STEREO TRACK

PETITE FLEUR

(LITTLE FLOWER)

BY SIDNEY BECHET

E♭ VERSION

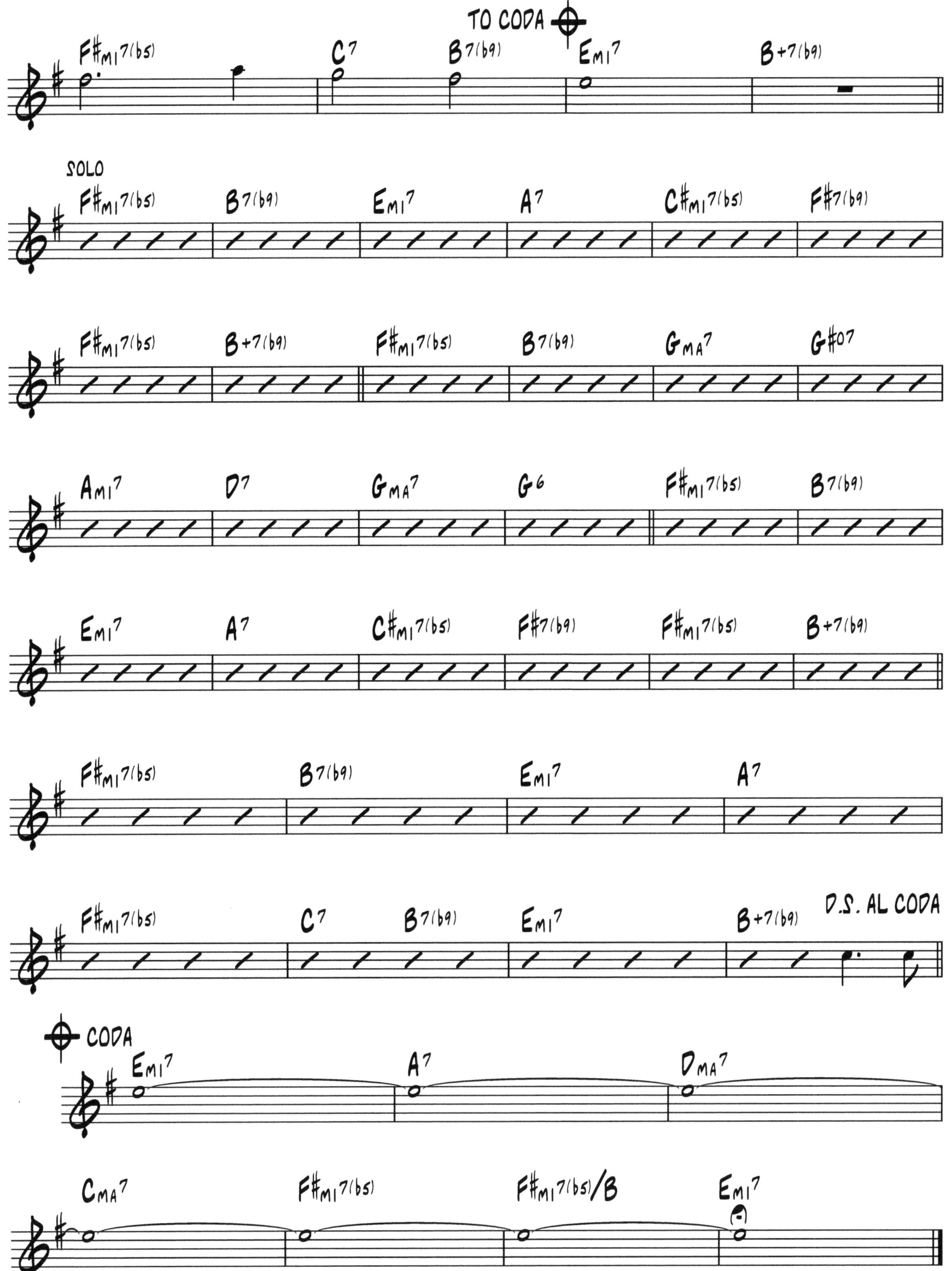
TO CODA
F#MI7(b5)
C7
B7(b9)
EMI7
B+7(b9)
SOLO
F#MI7(b5)
B7(b9)
EMI7
A7
C#MI7(b5)
F#7(b9)
F#MI7(b5)
B+7(b9)
F#MI7(b5)
B7(b9)
GMA7
G#o7
AMI7
D7
GMA7
G6
F#MI7(b5)
B7(b9)
EMI7
A7
C#MI7(b5)
F#7(b9)
F#MI7(b5)
B+7(b9)
F#MI7(b5)
B7(b9)
EMI7
A7
F#MI7(b5)
C7
B7(b9)
EMI7
B+7(b9)
D.S. AL CODA
CODA
EMI7
A7
DMA7
CMA7
F#MI7(b5)
F#MI7(b5)/B
EMI7

CD

1: SPLIT TRACK/MELODY
2: FULL STEREO TRACK

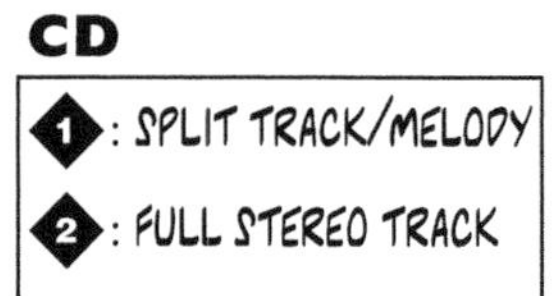

BIM-BOM

WORDS AND MUSIC BY
JOAO GILBERTO

Eb VERSION

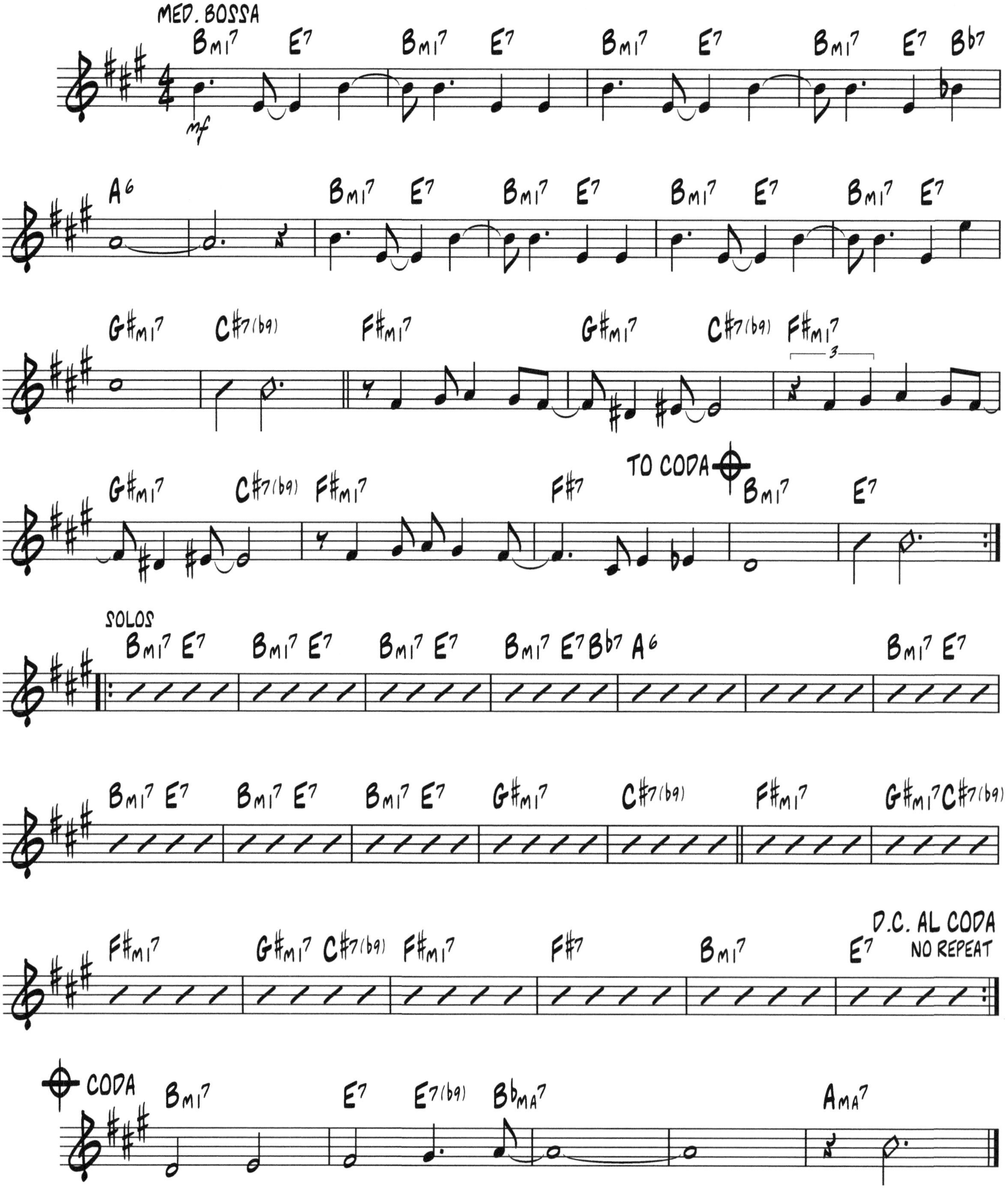

MED. BOSSA
Bmi7 E7 Bmi7 E7 Bmi7 E7 Bmi7 E7 Bb7
mf
A6 Bmi7 E7 Bmi7 E7 Bmi7 E7 Bmi7 E7
G#mi7 C#7(b9) F#mi7 G#mi7 C#7(b9) F#mi7
3
G#mi7 C#7(b9) F#mi7 F#7
TO CODA
Bmi7 E7
SOLOS
Bmi7 E7 Bmi7 E7 Bmi7 E7 Bmi7 E7 Bb7 A6 Bmi7 E7
Bmi7 E7 Bmi7 E7 Bmi7 E7 G#mi7 C#7(b9) F#mi7 G#mi7 C#7(b9)
F#mi7 G#mi7 C#7(b9) F#mi7 F#7 Bmi7 E7
D.C. AL CODA
NO REPEAT
CODA
Bmi7 E7 E7(b9) BbMA7 AMA7

BIM-BOM

CD
1 : SPLIT TRACK/MELODY
2 : FULL STEREO TRACK
C VERSION
WORDS AND MUSIC BY
JOAO GILBERTO
MED. BOSSA
DMI7 G7 DMI7 G7 DMI7 G7 DMI7 G7 Db7
mf
C6 DMI7 G7 DMI7 G7 DMI7 G7 DMI7 G7
BMI7 E7(b9) AMI7 BMI7 E7(b9) AMI7
3
BMI7 E7(b9) AMI7 A7
TO CODA
DMI7 G7
SOLOS
DMI7 G7 DMI7 G7 DMI7 G7 DMI7 G7 Db7 C6 DMI7 G7
DMI7 G7 DMI7 G7 DMI7 G7 BMI7 E7(b9) AMI7 BMI7 E7(b9)
AMI7 BMI7 E7(b9) AMI7 A7 DMI7 G7
D.C. AL CODA
NO REPEAT
CODA
DMI7 G7 G7(b9) DbMA7 CMA7

BOSSA ANTIGUA

BY PAUL DESMOND

Bbmi7 Eb7 Cmi7 Fmi7
Bbmi7 Eb7 Abma7 F+7
TO CODA
SOLO
Bbmi7 Eb7 Cmi7 Fmi7 Bbmi7
1. Eb7
Cmi7 F7
2. Dmi7 G7 Cma7 Ami7
Dmi7 G7 Emi7 Ami7 Dmi7 G7
Cmi7 F7 Bbmi7 Eb7 Cmi7 Fmi7
D.S. AL CODA
Bbmi7 Eb7 Abma7 Bbmi7 Eb7
CODA
Bbmi7 Eb7 Bbmi7 Eb7 Cmi7 F+7 Cmi7 F+7
Bbmi7 Eb7 Bbmi7 Eb7 Abma7

CD

5: SPLIT TRACK/MELODY
6: FULL STEREO TRACK

ESTATE

MUSIC BY BRUNO MARTINO
LYRICS BY BRUNO BRIGHETTI

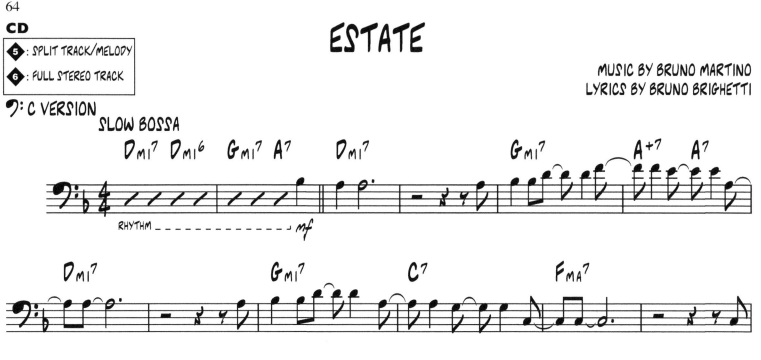

𝄢: C VERSION

SLOW BOSSA

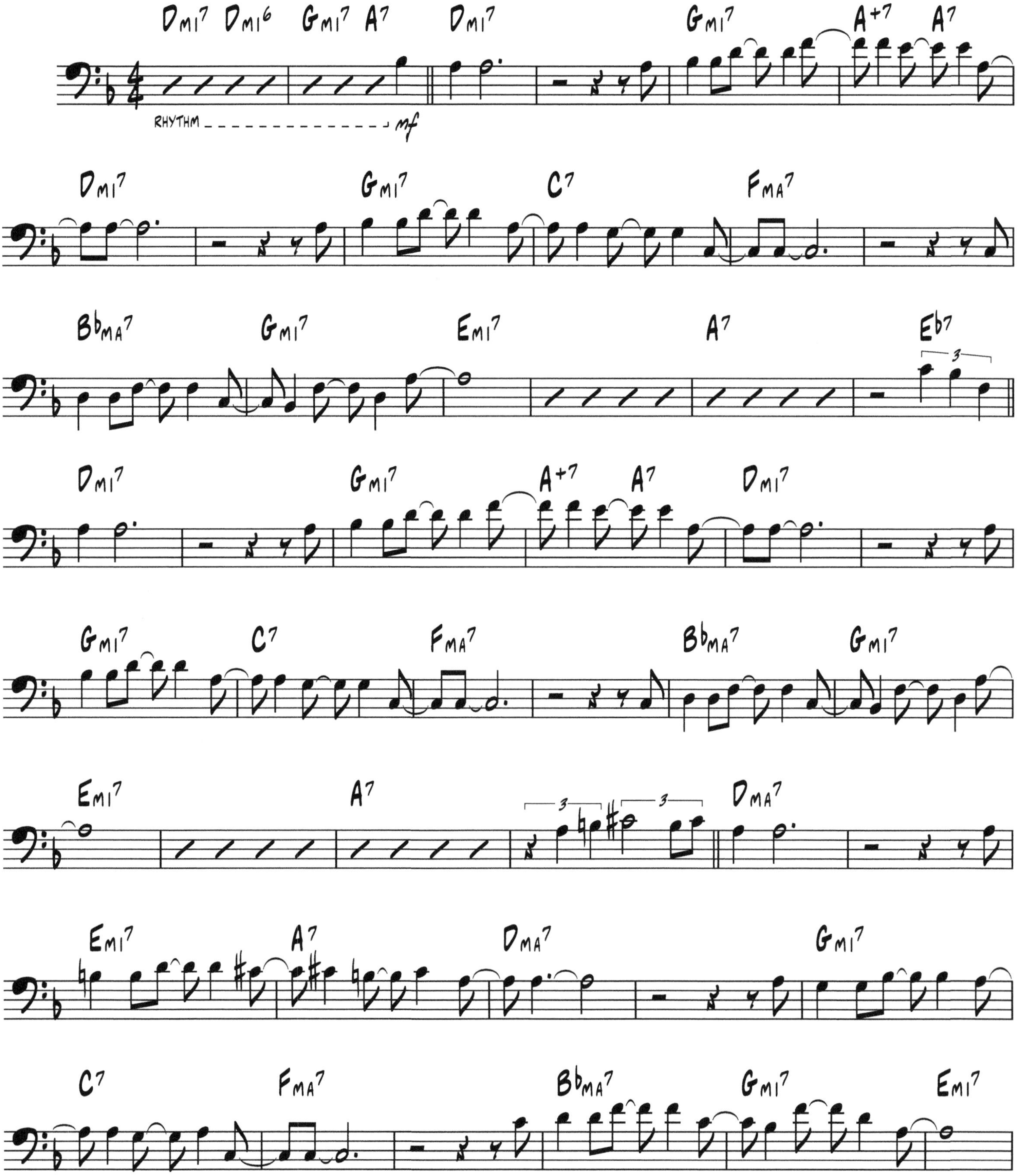

Dmi7 Dmi6 Gmi7 A7 Dmi7 Gmi7 A+7 A7

RHYTHM mf

Dmi7 Gmi7 C7 Fma7

Bbma7 Gmi7 Emi7 A7 Eb7

Dmi7 Gmi7 A+7 A7 Dmi7

Gmi7 C7 Fma7 Bbma7 Gmi7

Emi7 A7 Dma7

Emi7 A7 Dma7 Gmi7

C7 Fma7 Bbma7 Gmi7 Emi7

A7 Eb7 DMI7 GMI7
A+7 A7 DMI7 GMI7 C7
FMA7 BbMA7 GMI7 EMI7
A7 Eb7 DMI7 DMI6 GMI7 A7
DMI7 DMI6 BbMA7 GMI7 Eb7
SOLO
DMA7 EMI7
A7 DMA7 GMI7 C7 FMA7 BbMA7
GMI7 EMI7 A7 Eb7 DMI7 GMI7
A+7 A7 DMI7 GMI7 C7 FMA7 BbMA7
GMI7 EMI7 A7 Eb7 DMI7 DMI6 GMI7
A7 DMI7 DMI6 GMI7 A7 DMI7

CD

A FELICIDADE

WORDS AND MUSIC BY VINICIUS DE MORAES, ANDRE SALVET AND ANTONIO CARLOS JOBIM

C VERSION

FAST LATIN

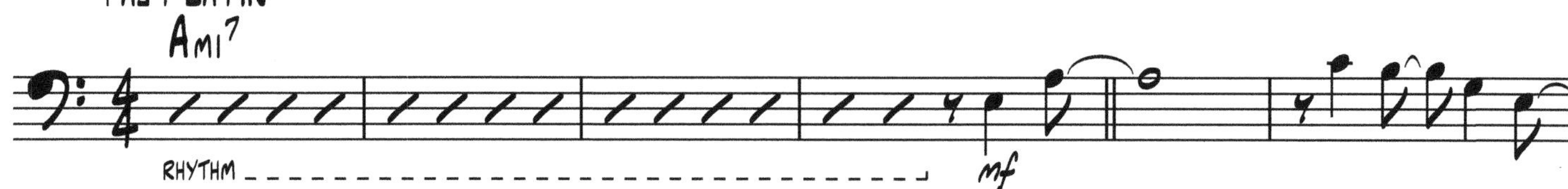

Emi7 A7 Dmi7 G7(b9) Ami7 Ami7/G D7/F#
TO CODA
Dmi7/F Ami7 Bmi7(b5) E+7(b9) Ami7
SOLO
Emi7 B7(b9) Emi7 A7 Dmi7 G7
Cma7 Bmi7(b5) E7(b9) Ami7 Ab7 Gmi7 Gb7
Fma7 Bb7 Ami7 D7 Ami7 Bmi7 E+7(b9) Ami7
G7sus G7 Cma7 F7 Cma7 Gmi7 C7
Fma7 Dmi7 G7 C6/9 F#mi7(b5)
B7(b9) Emi7 A7 Dmi7 G7(b9) Ami7 Ami7/G D7/F# Dmi7/F
D.S. AL CODA
CODA
PLAY 3X'S
Ami7 Bmi7(b5) E+7(b9) Ami7 G7sus G7 Ami7
Bmi7(b5) E+7(b9)
1., 2.
Ami7
3.
Ami7

CD
9 : SPLIT TRACK/MELODY
10 : FULL STEREO TRACK
FLAMINGO
LYRIC BY ED ANDERSON
MUSIC BY TED GROUYA
C VERSION
MED. BOSSA
Ab7SUS
G7SUS
G7(b9)
RHYTHM
mf
CMA7 DMI7 G+7 CMI7 F7SUS F7
Ab7 G7SUS G7(b9) 1. CMA7 G7SUS G7(b9)
2. C6 GMI7 C+7 FMI7 Bb7
Eb6/9 E07 FMI7 Bb7 /Ab
G7SUS G7(b9) G+7(b9) CMA7 DMI7 G+7
CMI7 Gb7 F7SUS F7 Ab7 G7SUS G7(b9)
TO CODA

CMA7
G7SUS
G7(b9)
SOLO
CMA7
DMI7
G+7
CMI7
F7SUS
F7
Ab7
G7SUS
G7(b9)
1.
CMA7
G7SUS
G7(b9)
2.
C6
GMI7
C+7
FMI7
Bb7
Eb6/9
E07
FMI7
Bb7
/Ab
G7SUS
G7(b9)
G+7(b9)
CMA7
DMI7
G+7
CMI7
Gb7
F7SUS
F7
Ab7
G7SUS
G7(b9)
CMA7
GMI7
C+7
D.S. AL CODA
CODA
CMA7
Bb7
CMA7
Bb7
CMA7
Bb7
CMA7

CD
11 : SPLIT TRACK/MELODY
12 : FULL STEREO TRACK
C VERSION
FRENESÍ
WORDS AND MUSIC BY
ALBERTO DOMINGUEZ
MEDIUM BOSSA
F+7 N.C.
Bbmi7 Eb7 Bbmi7 Eb7 Bbmi7 Eb7
mf
Bbmi7 Eb7 Abma7 Bbmi6 Eb7
1. Ab6 Ab6 G+7(b9) Gbma7 F+7 N.C.
3
2. Ab6 N.C. Cma7
Db7 Cma7 C6 N.C.
Cma7 Fmi7 Bb7 Bbmi7 Eb7 N.C.
3
Bbmi7 Eb7 Bbmi7 Eb7 Bbmi7 Eb7
Bbmi7 Eb7 Abma7 TO CODA Bbmi7 Eb7

SOLO
Ab6
Ab6 G+7(b9) Gbma7
F+7
SOLO BREAK
Bbmi7
Eb7
Bbmi7
Eb7
Bbmi7
Eb7
Bbmi7
Eb7
Abma7
Bbmi6
Eb7
1. Ab6
Ab6 G+7(b9) Gbma7
F+7
2. Ab6
Cma7
Db7
Cma7
C6
Cma7
Fmi7
Bb7
Bbmi7
Eb7
Bbmi7 Eb7
Bbmi7 Eb7
Bbmi7 Eb7
Bbmi7 Eb7
Abma7
Bbmi7 Eb7
Ab6
Ab6 G+7(b9) Gbma7
F+7 N.C.
D.S. AL CODA
TAKE REPEAT
CODA
Bbmi7
A9(#11)
Abma7

CD

13 : SPLIT TRACK/MELODY

14 : FULL STEREO TRACK

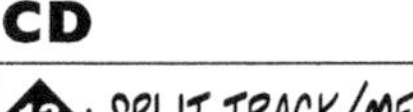

HO-BA-LA-LA

WORDS AND MUSIC BY NORMAN GIMBEL
AND JOAO GILBERTO

C VERSION

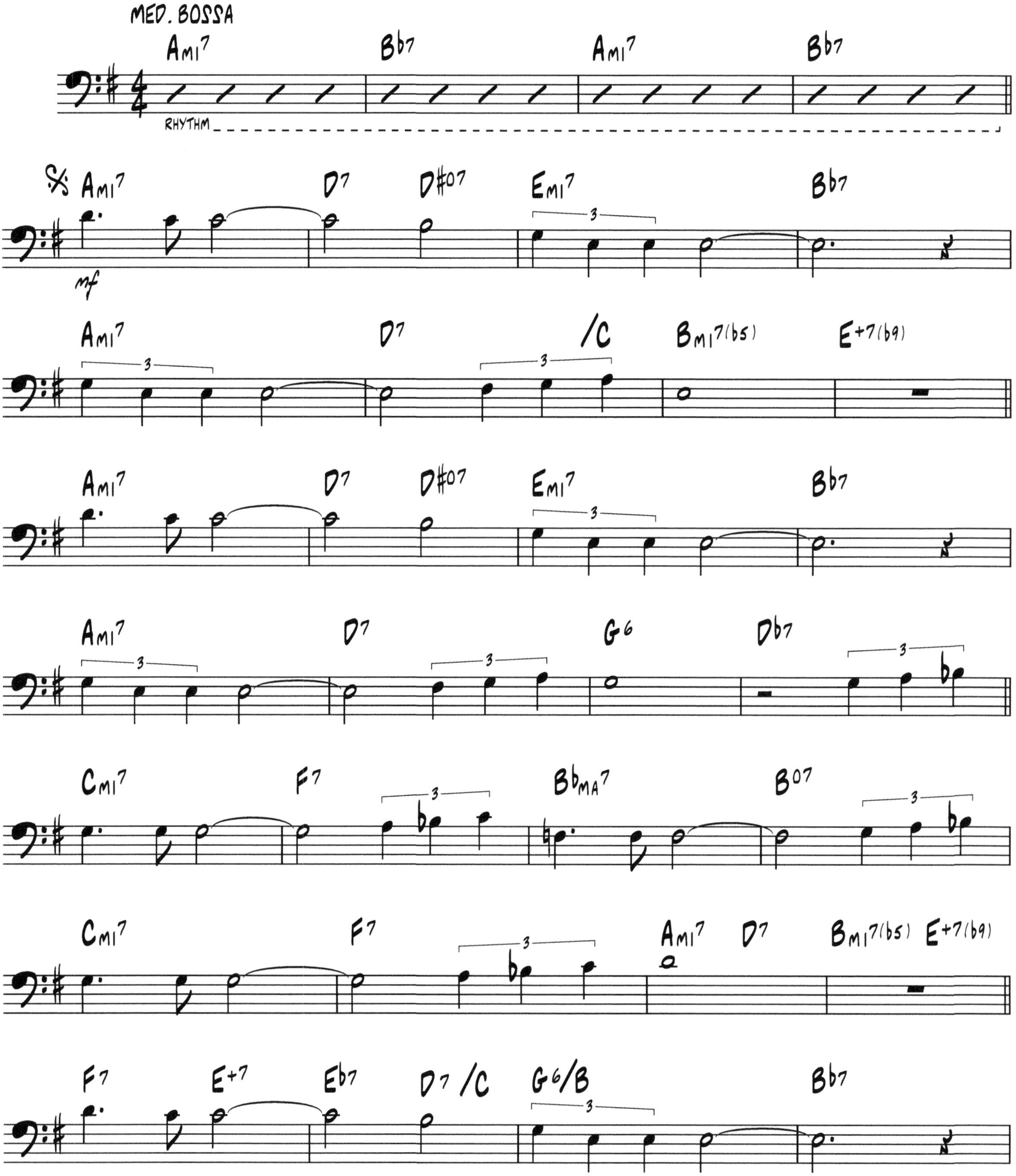

MED. BOSSA
AMI7 B♭7 AMI7 B♭7
RHYTHM
AMI7 D7 D#°7 EMI7 B♭7
mf
AMI7 D7 /C BMI7(♭5) E+7(♭9)
AMI7 D7 D#°7 EMI7 B♭7
AMI7 D7 G6 D♭7
CMI7 F7 B♭MA7 B°7
CMI7 F7 AMI7 D7 BMI7(♭5) E+7(♭9)
F7 E+7 E♭7 D7 /C G6/B B♭7

AMI7
D7
TO CODA
G6
BMI7(b5) E+7(b9)
SOLO
AMI7
D7
D#o7
EMI7
Bb7
AMI7
D7
1.
BMI7(b5)
E+7(b9)
2.
G6
Db7
CMI7
F7
BbMA7
Bo7
CMI7
F7
AMI7
D7
BMI7(b5)
E+7(b9)
AMI7
D7
D#o7
EMI7
Bb7
AMI7
D7
G6
Bb7
D.S. AL CODA
CODA
CMA7
Bb7
CMA7
Bb7
CMA7
Bb7
CMA7
Bb7
GMA7
RIT.

CD

15 : SPLIT TRACK/MELODY

16 : FULL STEREO TRACK

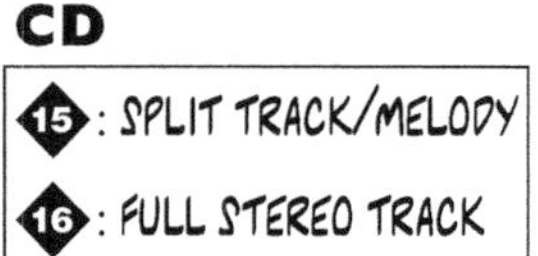

MENINA FLOR

WORDS BY MARIA TOLEDO
MUSIC BY LUIZ BONFA

?: C VERSION

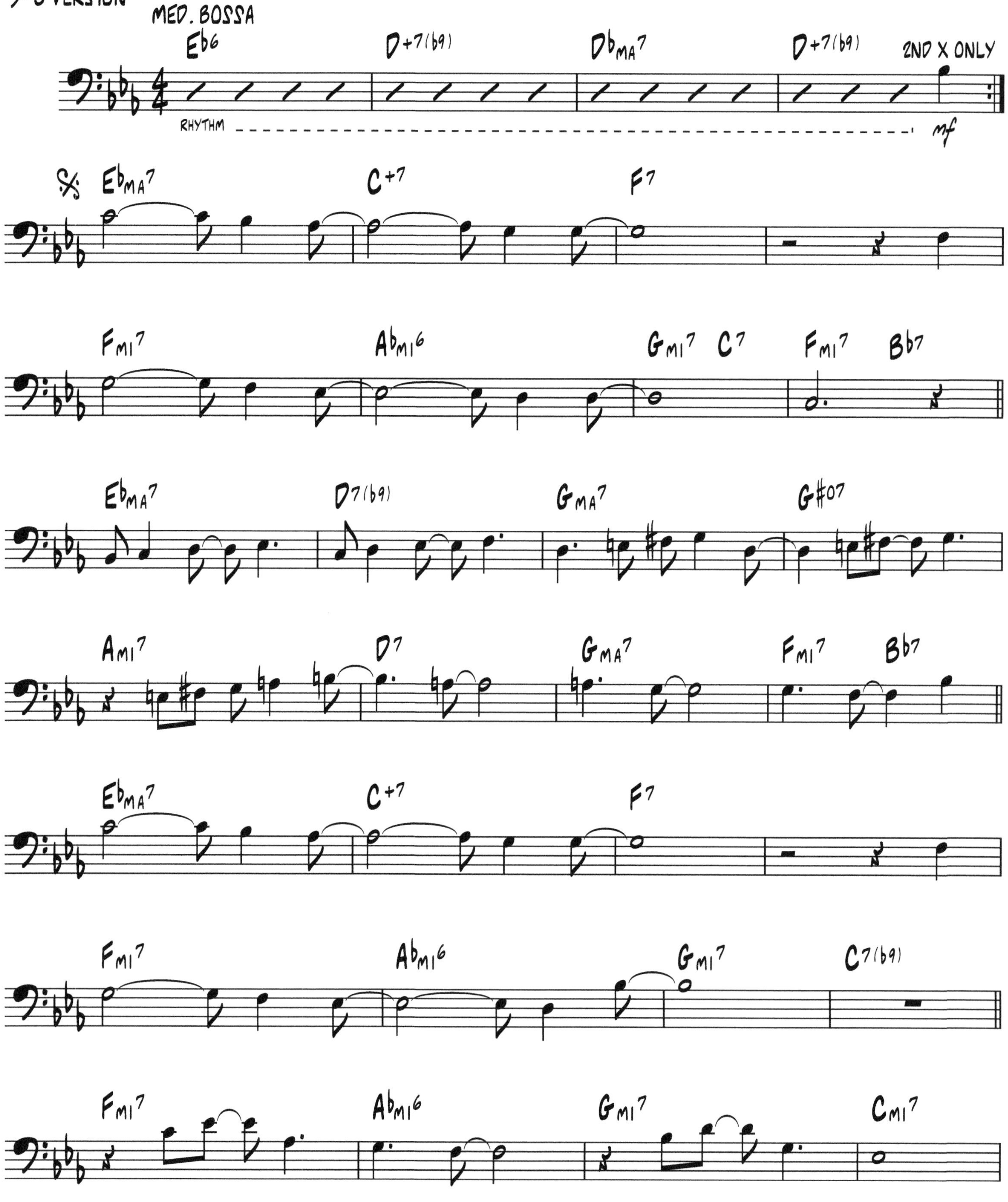

MED. BOSSA
Eb6 D+7(b9) DbMA7 D+7(b9) 2ND X ONLY
RHYTHM
mf
EbMA7 C+7 F7
FMI7 AbMI6 GMI7 C7 FMI7 Bb7
EbMA7 D7(b9) GMA7 G#o7
AMI7 D7 GMA7 FMI7 Bb7
EbMA7 C+7 F7
FMI7 AbMI6 GMI7 C7(b9)
FMI7 AbMI6 GMI7 CMI7

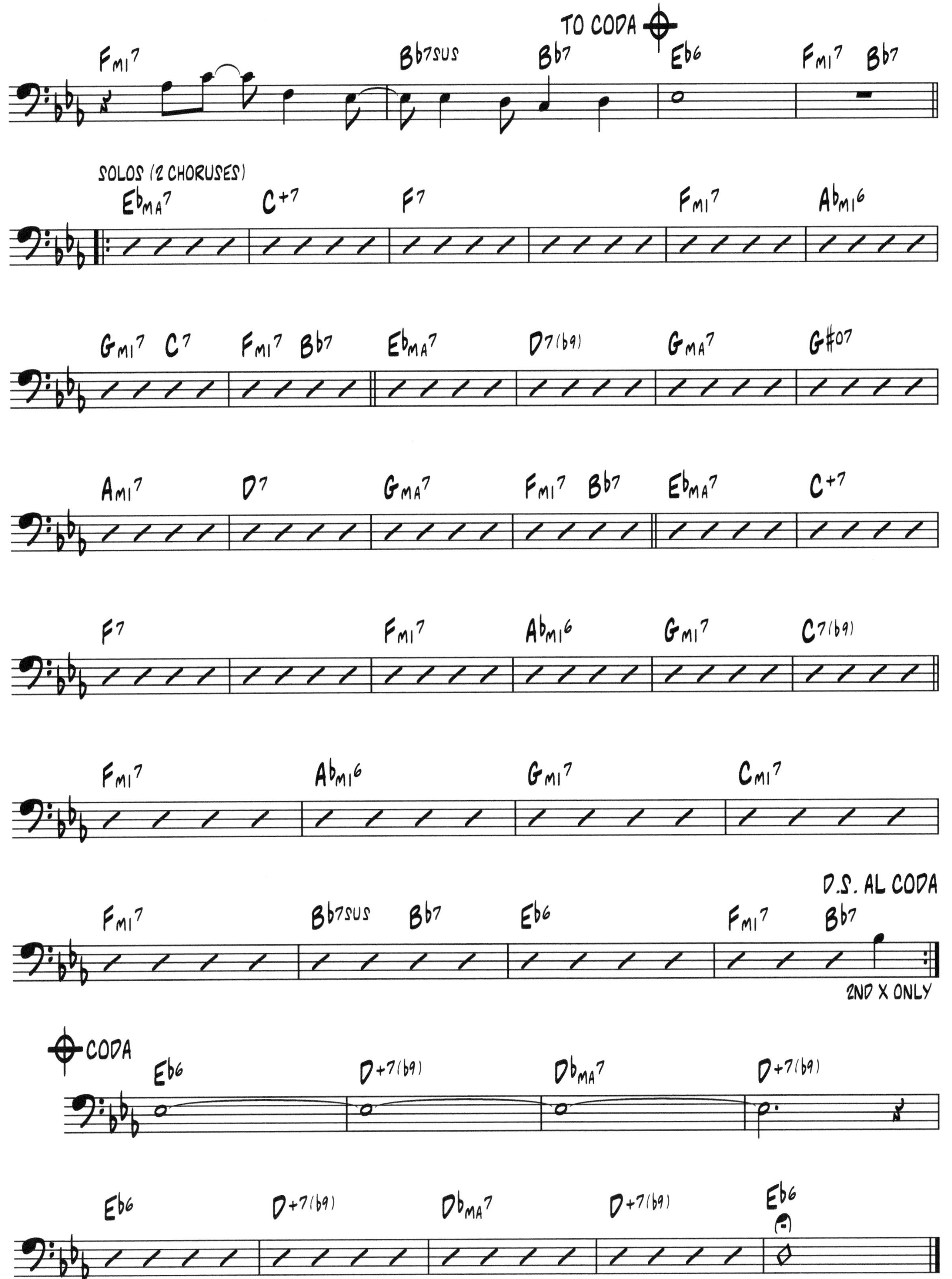

TO CODA
FMI7
Bb7SUS
Bb7
Eb6
FMI7
Bb7
SOLOS (2 CHORUSES)
EbMA7
C+7
F7
FMI7
AbMI6
GMI7
C7
FMI7
Bb7
EbMA7
D7(b9)
GMA7
G#07
AMI7
D7
GMA7
FMI7
Bb7
EbMA7
C+7
F7
FMI7
AbMI6
GMI7
C7(b9)
FMI7
AbMI6
GMI7
CMI7
D.S. AL CODA
FMI7
Bb7SUS
Bb7
Eb6
FMI7
Bb7
2ND X ONLY
CODA
Eb6
D+7(b9)
DbMA7
D+7(b9)
Eb6
D+7(b9)
DbMA7
D+7(b9)
Eb6

CD

O PATO
(THE DUCK)

WORDS AND MUSIC BY JAYME SILVA AND NEUZA TEIXIERA
ENGLISH LYRIC BY JON HENDRICKS

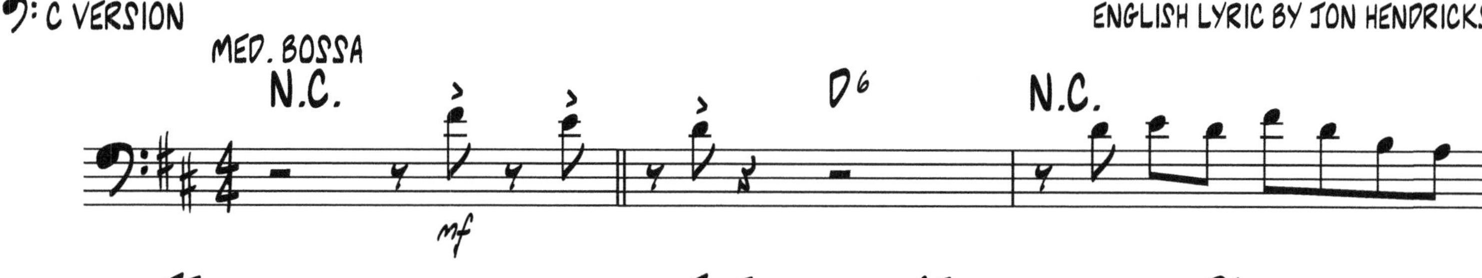

A7
DMA7
E7
TO CODA
Eb7
D6
SOLO BREAK
SOLOS (2 FULL CHORUSES)
D6
E7
EMI7
A7
D6
AMI7
D7
GMA7
E7
A7SUS
DMA7
AMI7
D7
GMA7
C7
D6
GMA7
C7
D6
GMA7
DMA7/F#
E7
A7
DMA7
E7
Eb7(#9)
D6
D.S. AL CODA
CODA
Eb7
Bb+7
A7(b9)
D6

19 : SPLIT TRACK/MELODY
20 : FULL STEREO TRACK

C VERSION

PETITE FLEUR
(LITTLE FLOWER)

BY SIDNEY BECHET

SLOW BOSSA

Gmi9 C7 Fma7 Ebma7 Ami7(b5) D+7(b9)

RHYTHM

mf

Ami7(b5) D7(b9) Gmi7 C7

Emi7(b5) A7(b9) Ami7(b5) D+7(b9)

Ami7(b5) D7(b9) Bbma7 B°7

Cmi7 F7 Bbma7 Bb6

Ami7(b5) D7(b9) Gmi7 C7

Emi7(b5) A7(b9) Ami7(b5) D+7(b9)

Ami7(b5) D7(b9) Gmi7 C7

TO CODA
AMI7(b5)
Eb7
D7(b9)
GMI7
D+7(b9)
SOLO
AMI7(b5)
D7(b9)
GMI7
C7
EMI7(b5)
A7(b9)
AMI7(b5)
D+7(b9)
AMI7(b5)
D7(b9)
BbMA7
B°7
CMI7
F7
BbMA7
Bb6
AMI7(b5)
D7(b9)
GMI7
C7
EMI7(b5)
A7(b9)
AMI7(b5)
D+7(b9)
AMI7(b5)
D7(b9)
GMI7
C7
AMI7(b5)
Eb7
D7(b9)
GMI7
D+7(b9)
D.S. AL CODA
CODA
GMI7
C7
FMA7
EbMA7
AMI7(b5)
AMI7(b5)/D
GMI7

Presenting the Hal Leonard JAZZ PLAY-ALONG® SERIES

1. DUKE ELLINGTON
00841644 $16.95

1A. MAIDEN VOYAGE/ALL BLUES
00843158 $15.99

2. MILES DAVIS
00841645 $16.95

3. THE BLUES
00841646 $16.99

4. JAZZ BALLADS
00841691 $16.99

5. BEST OF BEBOP
00841689 $16.99

6. JAZZ CLASSICS WITH EASY CHANGES
00841690 $16.99

7. ESSENTIAL JAZZ STANDARDS
00843000 $16.99

8. ANTONIO CARLOS JOBIM AND THE ART OF THE BOSSA NOVA
00843001 $16.95

9. DIZZY GILLESPIE
00843002 $16.99

10. DISNEY CLASSICS
00843003 $16.99

11. RODGERS AND HART – FAVORITES
00843004 $16.99

12. ESSENTIAL JAZZ CLASSICS
00843005 $16.99

13. JOHN COLTRANE
00843006 $16.95

14. IRVING BERLIN
00843007 $15.99

15. RODGERS & HAMMERSTEIN
00843008 $15.99

16. COLE PORTER
00843009 $15.95

17. COUNT BASIE
00843010 $16.95

18. HAROLD ARLEN
00843011 $15.95

19. COOL JAZZ
00843012 $15.95

20. CHRISTMAS CAROLS
00843080 $14.95

21. RODGERS AND HART – CLASSICS
00843014 $14.95

22. WAYNE SHORTER
00843015 $16.95

23. LATIN JAZZ
00843016 $16.95

24. EARLY JAZZ STANDARDS
00843017 $14.95

25. CHRISTMAS JAZZ
00843018 $16.95

26. CHARLIE PARKER
00843019 $16.95

27. GREAT JAZZ STANDARDS
00843020 $15.99

28. BIG BAND ERA
00843021 $15.99

29. LENNON AND McCARTNEY
00843022 $16.95

30. BLUES' BEST
00843023 $15.99

31. JAZZ IN THREE
00843024 $15.99

32. BEST OF SWING
00843025 $15.99

33. SONNY ROLLINS
00843029 $15.95

34. ALL TIME STANDARDS
00843030 $15.99

35. BLUESY JAZZ
00843031 $15.99

36. HORACE SILVER
00843032 $16.99

37. BILL EVANS
00843033 $16.95

38. YULETIDE JAZZ
00843034 $16.95

39. "ALL THE THINGS YOU ARE" & MORE JEROME KERN SONGS
00843035 $15.99

40. BOSSA NOVA
00843036 $15.99

41. CLASSIC DUKE ELLINGTON
00843037 $16.99

42. GERRY MULLIGAN – FAVORITES
00843038 $16.99

43. GERRY MULLIGAN – CLASSICS
00843039 $16.95

44. OLIVER NELSON
00843040 $16.95

45. JAZZ AT THE MOVIES
00843041 $15.99

46. BROADWAY JAZZ STANDARDS
00843042 $15.99

47. CLASSIC JAZZ BALLADS
00843043 $15.99

48. BEBOP CLASSICS
00843044 $16.99

49. MILES DAVIS – STANDARDS
00843045 $16.95

50. GREAT JAZZ CLASSICS
00843046 $15.99

51. UP-TEMPO JAZZ
00843047 $15.99

52. STEVIE WONDER
00843048 $15.95

53. RHYTHM CHANGES
00843049 $15.99

54. "MOONLIGHT IN VERMONT" & OTHER GREAT STANDARDS
00843050 $15.99

55. BENNY GOLSON
00843052 $15.95

56. "GEORGIA ON MY MIND" & OTHER SONGS BY HOAGY CARMICHAEL
00843056 $15.99

57. VINCE GUARALDI
00843057 $16.99

58. MORE LENNON AND McCARTNEY
00843059 $15.99

59. SOUL JAZZ
00843060 $15.99

60. DEXTER GORDON
00843061 $15.95

61. MONGO SANTAMARIA
00843062 $15.95

62. JAZZ-ROCK FUSION
00843063 $14.95

63. CLASSICAL JAZZ
00843064 $14.95

64. TV TUNES
00843065 $14.95

65. SMOOTH JAZZ
00843066 $16.99

66. A CHARLIE BROWN CHRISTMAS
00843067 $16.99

67. CHICK COREA
00843068 $15.95

68. CHARLES MINGUS
00843069 $16.95

69. CLASSIC JAZZ
00843071 $15.99

70. THE DOORS
00843072 $14.95

71. COLE PORTER CLASSICS
00843073 $14.95

72. CLASSIC JAZZ BALLADS
00843074 $15.99

73. JAZZ/BLUES
00843075 $14.95

74. BEST JAZZ CLASSICS
00843076 $15.99

75. PAUL DESMOND
00843077 $14.95

76. BROADWAY JAZZ BALLADS
00843078 $15.99

77. JAZZ ON BROADWAY
00843079 $15.99

78. STEELY DAN
00843070 $14.99

79. MILES DAVIS – CLASSICS
00843081 $15.99

80. JIMI HENDRIX
00843083 $15.99

81. FRANK SINATRA – CLASSICS
00843084 $15.99

82. FRANK SINATRA – STANDARDS
00843085 $15.99

83. ANDREW LLOYD WEBBER
00843104 $14.95

84. BOSSA NOVA CLASSICS
00843105 $14.95

85. MOTOWN HITS
00843109 $14.95

86. BENNY GOODMAN
00843110 $14.95

87. DIXIELAND
00843111 $14.95

88. DUKE ELLINGTON FAVORITES
00843112 $14.95

89. IRVING BERLIN FAVORITES
00843113 $14.95

90. THELONIOUS MONK CLASSICS
00841262 $16.99

91. THELONIOUS MONK FAVORITES
00841263 $16.99

92. LEONARD BERNSTEIN
00450134 $15.99

93. DISNEY FAVORITES
00843142 $14.99

94. RAY
00843143 $14.99

95. JAZZ AT THE LOUNGE
00843144 $14.99

96. LATIN JAZZ STANDARDS
00843145 $14.99

97. MAYBE I'M AMAZED
00843148 $15.99

98. DAVE FRISHBERG
00843149 $15.99

99. SWINGING STANDARDS
00843150 $14.99

100. LOUIS ARMSTRONG
00740423 $15.99

101. BUD POWELL
00843152 $14.99

102. JAZZ POP
00843153 $14.99

103. ON GREEN DOLPHIN STREET & OTHER JAZZ CLASSICS
00843154 $14.99

104. ELTON JOHN
00843155 $14.99

105. SOULFUL JAZZ
00843151 $15.99

106. SLO' JAZZ
00843117 $14.99

107. MOTOWN CLASSICS
00843116 $14.99

108. JAZZ WALTZ
00843159 $15.99

109. OSCAR PETERSON
00843160 $15.99

110. JUST STANDARDS
00843161 $15.99

111. COOL CHRISTMAS
00843162 $15.99

114. MODERN JAZZ QUARTET FAVORITES
00843163 $15.99

115. THE SOUND OF MUSIC
00843164 $15.99

116. JACO PASTORIUS
00843165 $15.99

117. ANTONIO CARLOS JOBIM – MORE HITS
00843166 $15.99

118. BIG JAZZ STANDARDS COLLECTION
00843167 $27.50

119. JELLY ROLL MORTON
00843168 $15.99

120. J.S. BACH
00843169 $15.99

121. DJANGO REINHARDT
00843170 $15.99

122. PAUL SIMON
00843182 $16.99

123. BACHARACH & DAVID
00843185 $15.99

124. JAZZ-ROCK HORN HITS
00843186 $15.99

126. COUNT BASIE CLASSICS
00843157 $15.99